THE THIN BOOK OF ®

Smart People Skills

8 TOOLS FOR THE

Savvy Leader

Savvy Leaders Reviews

Fantastic guide for new people managers or managers who struggle with their emotional intelligence (EQ) skills. The TIPS are great for a quick revision and are perfect for busy managers. The fabulous thing about this book is that the skills that Katina teaches can be applied to all manner of interaction with people - not just who you manage or work with. I see great value in applying these skills to improve the interactions that I have with my three children.

Samantha Zammit, Director Transactional Partner Group, Microsoft Australia Pty Ltd

A concise easy to understand set of principles. You keep on finding yourself agreeing with the content. This book should be read annually by managers as part of the performance review process.

Colin Burns, Head of Treasury - BNP Paribas Sydney Branch

This is a remarkable book. It takes complex concepts and makes them accessible. It enables managers to be better leaders of people. It's the ideal guide for aspiring people managers and for established managers who are puzzled by people and who are looking for insight. There are many, many useful tips in this book. Not least is the section on process. This much neglected area in the popular literature is critical if managers are to affect long-term and meaningful change. It's a must read.

Peter May, Regional HR Director, EMEA, Deloitte

Contents

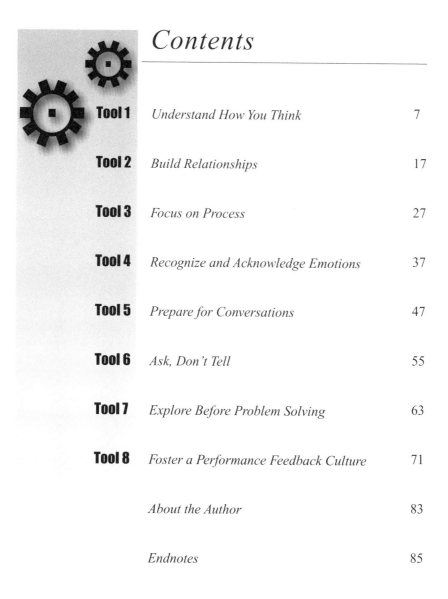

> *Why read this book?*

So often in the workplace, people who are immensely talented, highly driven and hard working fail to achieve the success they deserve. They progress well in their work up to a certain level where they seem to reach a plateau. They don't quite realize their potential, are unable to harness the potential of their teams, and find it difficult to gain full satisfaction from their working lives.

The disabling factor for these people, in my experience, is nearly always people skills — how to interact with, work with, and lead other people. Being able to create an environment that people want to work and excel in is becoming increasingly important. This book offers you succinct and useful tactics that will produce results toward your strategic goals. Applied consistently, these people skills will help you improve relationships and performance.

The information for this book comes from my more than two decades as a psychologist. I began witnessing the effectiveness of these people techniques during my very first experience as a business consultant. I was brought in to be a role-player at an assessment center for senior leaders, acting as a

disgruntled customer, a challenging direct report, and a demanding peer. Each senior leader had to role-play a new managing director on his/her first day on the job taking meetings with each of the three characters I was playing.

During the role-plays, I was often impressed with the managers' financial calculations, quick minds, and strategic solutions to the issues I presented. But in many cases this was not enough to gain my commitment or to address the issues. As a result, at the end of many role-plays, I would feel frustrated, not listened to, and sometimes angry. On the other hand, some role-plays left me feeling admiration for a leader who demonstrated both strong business acumen and great people skills. What were they doing differently? That is what this book teaches.

Since that first experience, I have worked with hundreds of knowledge workers and leaders and have found that they encounter similar patterns and frustrations in managing and influencing people. This book lays out the eight most common areas that impact your ability to influence and work with others. The tools summarized here describe recurring challenges and provide methods to overcome them. In live coaching sessions, you would experience first-hand 'a-ha' moments of insight; this book allows you to put yourself 'there' and derive a similar benefit.

Much of what you read here is available in other places, usually in much thicker books that require teasing out the critical messages. The value of the content presented in this Thin Book is in its short and realistic format. Whether the principles are new to you or are well-worn material, everyone can benefit from a potent and handy review of these tips — they are the foundation skills of savvy leaders.

A growing number of writers and thinkers in the field of leadership development discuss the critical impact of a leader's self-awareness and relationship skills on their ability to lead and apply basic business skills. My 23 years of experience working with people — as a coach, consultant, and psychotherapist — have shown me that positive transformations can happen in relationships when people are more aware of themselves.

This book is about achieving breakthroughs. Breakthroughs in peoples' performances can occur when relationships improve and people can have more honest and real conversations about their work. By understanding the subtle and not-so-subtle dynamics that happen between people — beginning with understanding your own behavior — you will become more aware of habits that may be holding you back from becoming a more savvy leader.

In our fast-paced lives there seems to be more and more emphasis on our outer lives and on 'doing.' Regard this book as an opportunity to slow down for a short time to go inward a bit, to honestly reflect on your habits and how you relate to others at work. To get the most out of this book, I suggest you read a chapter at a time, reflect and then practice one or two tips. If you do, I am sure you will reap benefits in your personal and professional relationships and in your own and your team's performance. Thank you for letting me be your coach and I'd love to hear how it goes.

Katina Cremona,
Athens, Greece
Kings Cross, Australia
katina@katinacremona.com

THIN BOOK PUBLISHING CO

Series Editor:
Sue Annis Hammond
(sue@thinbook.com)

Business Manager:
Rand Hammond
(rand@thinbook.com)

Designer:
Alisann Marshall
(alisann@thinbook.com)

Illustrator:
Keith Bendis
(bendis@taconic.net),
www.keithbendis.com

Author dedication:
For my parents,
Paul and Sylvia Cremona

ISBN: 978-0-9665373-8-3

Thin Book Publishing Co
86 SW Century Dr #446
Bend OR 97702
888.316.9544
541.382.7579
541.317.8606 (fax)
www.thinbook.com

Printed on recycled paper

Tool 1... Understand How You Think

A coaching client Robert told me he was putting off having a discussion with one of his direct reports, Pam. He needed to address the fact that she wasn't doing well in her position and wasn't eager to have the conversation.

What's stopping you from having a meeting with Pam?, I asked.

He responded sheepishly. *I don't want to upset her. I don't want a scene.*

How do you think you'll upset Pam? I probed, hoping to uncover the beliefs that Robert was operating from.

Because it's not going to be a nice discussion and she'll probably cry on me.

What makes you think that?

I don't know. I just don't want any emotional scenes.

What is it about emotional scenes you don't like?
Robert thought about this for a moment and then replied,
*They always end up badly and I don't want to risk that
happening.*

By the end of our conversation, Robert realized he was
operating from several beliefs that were contributing to his
reluctance to confront Pam. He believed there would be an
emotional scene, it would damage his relationship with Pam,
and that conflict should always be avoided. Once Robert's
thinking was revealed, we could then challenge his beliefs
to test whether they were actually true or helpful. For example, Robert decided that he needed to do some more
thinking about the value of conflict, exploring the notion that
it can be a positive experience rather than something to be
avoided. He also realized that he was assuming Pam would
react emotionally and that would damage his relationship
with her.

How We Think Has A Powerful Impact On Our Lives

Cognitive Behavioral Therapy is a very important and well-
researched branch of psychology. Pioneered by Albert Ellis[1]
and further developed by Aaron Beck,[2] it is based on the idea
that our thoughts influence how we feel, and that our feelings
affect how we think. How we think strongly affects most
aspects of our lives, including our behaviors, relationships,
work, and health. Some of our beliefs are conscious so we are
aware of them. For example, you might have a belief that you
can do anything you set your mind to. This belief would influence many aspects of your life: your confidence, your
willingness to take risks, how you relate to others. Many of the
other beliefs we hold are unconscious and operate outside our

awareness, yet their impact can be subtle and powerful. Without even realizing it, a leader might believe she can't trust others to do anything right. This unconscious belief can influence how much she is willing to delegate, how she relates to others, and, if she's doing too much on her own, her health.

Many researchers and psychologists continue to explore the link between our thinking and other aspects of our lives. Author Martin Seligman[3] writes that having an optimistic and hopeful thinking style can create better resistance against depression when challenging events occur, lead to better performance at work, and improve physical health. Barbara Fredrickson's[4] research into the effect of positive emotions — feeling grateful or upbeat, for instance — can broaden our thinking and build enduring benefits such as innovative ideas, novel actions and social connections. Her broaden-and-build theory refers to a mutually reinforcing spiral that can result in increased resilience, more creative and flexible thinking and ultimately, the ability to function at higher levels. On the other side of the spectrum, researchers have found that negative moods can help the brain focus on potential errors and distortions.[5] Knowing how moods can affect the creative or problem-solving process can help leaders set the right environment for a task or match a task to people's moods. If problem solving is needed, create a sense of urgency; if creativity is needed, use humor and fun.

How Thinking Develops And Changes

How we think changes throughout our lives. We develop, refine, or change our beliefs based on life experience, teachers, friends, colleagues, books we read, and media we are exposed to. Many of our beliefs are constructive and helpful, while others may have restricting or negative influences. Robert's situation illustrates how thinking, feeling, and behavior influence

> The discrepancy
between our
expectations and how
others actually
behave has a huge
influence on many
working relationships.

each other in reciprocal ways. Our behavior can change how we feel. For example, two managers might form an initial impression that they don't like or respect each other and avoid getting to know each other. When they eventually talk, they find they feel more positive about each other. By changing their behavior from not talking to talking, they change the way they think and feel about each other. By taking the time to identify his underlying beliefs in relation to Pam, Robert could decide to think and feel differently about meeting with her, and consequently choose a different behavior.

The Importance Of Knowing What You Think

Imagine that you believe your boss thinks you are incompetent. Think about how this might influence your feelings and behaviors at work. Now, imagine that you begin to feel increasingly negative about coming to work and interpret what your boss says as evidence that she really does think you're incompetent. Your boss, in turn, begins to be affected by your actions, judges you more negatively, and acts accordingly. You can see how this cycle can spiral, in either a positive or negative direction.[6]

This dynamic of how our expectations can influence how others behave has been widely researched in hundreds of studies[7] and is commonly referred to as the Self-Fulfilling Prophecy or Pygmalion Effect. It is important to understand how our thinking can co-create the dynamics in our relationships. Your thinking influences many aspects of your working life including:

YOUR RELATIONSHIPS. The types and number of beliefs we have about relationships are endless. They include beliefs about intimacy, conflict, support, feedback, trust, quantity and quality of contact, and emotions. For example, *Meetings are a waste of time and Emotions have no place at work* are two commonly held beliefs that could be operating in any given workplace. In our working relationships, there are beliefs about what leaders, colleagues, and direct reports should do. We often assume that others think the same way we do. The discrepancy between our expectations and how others actually behave has a huge influence on many working relationships. What do you think others should do that they are not doing? How aware are they about your expectations of them?

YOUR GENERAL HAPPINESS AND HEALTH. Some leaders believe they can maintain good personal relationships and health while working unrealistic hours and traveling most of the year. Which of your beliefs related to your work affect your happiness or health positively or negatively?

YOUR APPROACH TO PROBLEM SOLVING. Our beliefs can expand or limit the way we approach problem solving and tasks. Consider phrases like: *We always do that … , You should always… , It can't be done … .* What beliefs do you hold that expand or limit people's ability to create and think in new ways?

YOUR CONFIDENCE LEVELS. I have met many confidence-challenged employees. Some beliefs we've uncovered where confidence levels are fragile include the following: *I should be good at … , I'm never good enough, If I don't please everyone, I won't be liked.*

One manager in particular lived by this last belief to the point that he was exhausted from doing his job and helping his colleagues and direct reports with theirs. This belief contributed to his inability to say no to requests for his help. What beliefs do you hold that build or inhibit your confidence levels?

Identify Your Thinking

It is particularly important to identify aspects of our thinking that we may not be aware of. Here are three ways to become more aware of your thinking:

1. ASK YOURSELF WHAT YOU'RE THINKING. Catching fleeting thoughts can lead to discovering the beliefs that lie behind them. For example, a manager might think: *My direct reports are so incompetent, why can't they think for themselves?* Possible beliefs that may be operating in this scenario are: *They should know what I want them to do, People should think like I do, and They should do things the way I would.*

2. IDENTIFY HOW YOU ARE FEELING ESPECIALLY WHEN YOU DON'T FEEL GOOD. You may regularly feel frustrated. Asking yourself why you might be feeling this way can be another way to uncover your thinking around an issue. You might feel frustrated and angry every time you are interrupted by one of your direct reports. Maybe you believe that you shouldn't be interrupted during a certain period and didn't tell anyone this, or that people should be independent and not need your help.

3. EXAMINE YOUR BEHAVIORS. For example, Martin finds himself socializing at work far more often than he'd like. He goes to client events, goes drinking with his work mates on Friday nights, and often attends work dinners. He would prefer to be home with his family and often feels resentment and dread when another function comes up. He finally asks himself why he's going to these events and identifies two beliefs: *I should socialize at work and I'm a bad employee if I don't go to every function.*

Challenge Your Thinking

Once you've identified a belief, you can challenge or dispute it.

ASK YOURSELF SOME OF THE FOLLOWING QUESTIONS:

- *Is this true?*
- *Is it that important?*
- *Where did I get this idea?*
- *What's the worst thing that would happen if I did or didn't do that?*

- *Is this a realistic point of view?*
- *How might I be expecting others to think, feel, or behave like me?*
- *How might I be expecting others to read my mind?*
- *What assumptions am I operating from? About others? About myself?*
- *What assumptions would be more helpful for me to operate from?*
- *How much are my feelings helping me do what I need to get done?*

The manager constantly interrupted by her direct reports might need to rethink her beliefs by asking herself some of these questions: *Is it realistic to expect not to be interrupted if I haven't made it clear that I don't want to be? Given the present skill levels of my direct reports, is it fair for me to expect them not to ask for help? How is my frustration helping them or me? What assumptions are operating on both sides that are contributing to this situation?*

Some beliefs involve unrealistic expectations. Expectations that people will be competent and mature are totally reasonable, but expecting these qualities from all people all the time will lead to frustration, blame, and disappointment. Are you asking for perfection? Match your expectations with the realities of human performance and human nature. Great leaders understand their own thinking, feeling, and behaviors in relation to various people and situations. An increasing number of writers in the field of leadership development stress the importance of leaders' understanding and managing themselves. Authors Hogan and Warrenfelz,[8] for example, suggest that how one manages oneself has implications for all other aspects of leadership performance and that the most important area leaders need to be educated in is human nature — in particular, their own.

> **>** An increasing number of writers in the field of leadership development stress the importance of leaders' understanding and managing themselves.

UNDERSTANDING HOW YOU THINK

❶ **KEEP ASKING YOURSELF WHY.** To uncover beliefs, keep asking yourself why. *Why do I think that? Why is that an issue?* Keep asking until you get to a deeper level of thinking within yourself. Then challenge your beliefs. If, like Robert, you find yourself avoiding something, ask yourself why.

Let's say you relate to the frustrated manager who bristles over being interrupted.

ASK YOURSELF WHY.

- *I never seem to have time to get through my own work. Why?*
- *Because I keep getting interrupted by my staff. Why?*
- *They knock at my door and ask me questions. Why?*
- *They need my help and I have an open-door policy. Why?*
- *Because I think it's important to be available for my staff. Why?*
- *They might think I don't care and I'm never around. So what's the belief?*
- *I should be available all the time for my staff. Now challenge this belief:*
- *Is this actually true?*
- *Is it realistic for you to be able to do the work that requires no interruption?*
- *How could you make some uninterrupted time for yourself?*
- *How do you think your staff would react?*
- *Do they really need your help for every question they ask? If so, why?*
- *How have you contributed to this situation?*
- *What assumptions are you making about your staff?*

❷ **GET A REALITY CHECK ON YOUR BELIEFS.** Besides asking why, it can also help to get a reality check. Ask trusted colleagues these types of questions: ***Am I being realistic in expecting or thinking this?*** Or ***what do you think about the***

way I responded? Or ***I reacted based on this premise (state the premise). Do you think that was reasonable?***

❸ **APPLY THESE IDEAS TO YOUR DIRECT REPORTS AND COLLEAGUES.** Help others to see what beliefs they may be operating from and how these affect how they feel and behave. This will help others learn to examine their own thinking and see the connection between their thinking, feeling, and behavior. You can ask helpful questions to consolidate this process of self-examination: ***What was your thinking or premise behind taking that action? What is important about this for you? What do you think would have happened if you hadn't done that? How aware are they of what you expect?***

❹ **MANAGING UPWARD: IDENTIFY AND CHALLENGE YOUR MANAGER'S THINKING.** Don't assume your manager has thought through all her ideas and priorities, or is aware of her thinking. By asking questions and challenging her thinking, you most likely will add more value to your discussions. Engaging with your manager in this way is an important aspect of managing upward.

❺ **VIRTUAL TEAMS: ARE YOU ASSUMING YOU KNOW HOW OTHERS THINK, FEEL, OR BEHAVE?** If so, stop yourself. Sometimes we go through whole scenarios in our heads about why someone has behaved in a certain way without ever asking the person involved. Managing this tendency is especially relevant for virtual teams, where it is often easier to make assumptions rather than clarifying what is actually going on. For example, when a team member hasn't called you back; you may assume he's not going to do what you asked him to do. It is usually worth waiting for time zones to be aligned to phone and clarify why others have decided to do something or have not responded to a call or email. The less we interact face-to-face with others, the more chance there can be of building up distorted assumptions and beliefs about them.

⑥ CROSS-CULTURAL TEAMS: IDENTIFY DIFFERENT CULTURAL ASSUMPTIONS AND BELIEFS.

In your conversations, inquire about and discuss how your colleagues' cultural differences might lead to seeing things differently. In a team meeting, write a list of 'shoulds' or expectations that people from different cultures hold about specific areas like motivation, performance appraisal, or aspects of communication. Look for generalizations, similarities, and differences. For example: *Direct reports should never contradict their boss* compared with *It's important to challenge your boss.* Besides asking people directly about their culture, several authors have done extensive research on working and managing within different cultures. Some of their books are referred to in the following chapters and the resources list at the end of this book.

We have looked at the first tool in getting to know more about how you and others think. Now that we've explored the importance of identifying and managing beliefs and assumptions, let's look at the second tool — building relationships. This tool will assist you to continue building an understanding of what people think about and what makes them tick.

⚙️ Tool 2...Build Relationships

At a leadership workshop I once facilitated, we were talking about the importance of knowing your direct reports as whole people.

Some workshop participants interpreted this to mean they had to talk about their private lives. They immediately felt uncomfortable with this idea and made their discomfort known with comments like *I keep work separate from home,* and *I don't want to know about their personal lives, and I don't tell them about mine.* People were concerned that knowing direct reports as whole people would take the focus away from getting the job done. Some people were also clear that they didn't want to be too friendly, too 'soft,' or 'touchy-feely' out of a fear that they would then not be able to be tough when they needed to be.

• • • **(>)** The very nature of work is 'relational' meaning there is some sort of relationship between you and the people you work with.

The very nature of work is 'relational' meaning there is some sort of relationship between you and the people you work with. And it is through these relationships that the work gets done. There are many types and levels of work relationships. You certainly don't have to be best friends with your direct reports or tell your colleagues about your innermost feelings; nor is this a guarantee of a constructive working relationship. What is important is having the skills to build relationships that boost people's strengths, motivation, and desire to have an impact at work. Building relationships requires three things: developing trust and openness, adapting your style to the style of others, and understanding others. In all of these, conversation is key.

To help you to think about whether or not you have an open, working relationship with your direct reports and peers, answer the following questions:

- Do you know what your employees/peers enjoy the most about their jobs?
- Are you aware of what motivates them, or what stresses them the most?
- Do you know what they appreciate most about you?
- Do you know what they really think of you as a leader?

If you can answer these questions, I'm guessing you have developed an honest and solid working relationship with your direct reports and peers. If you can't, consider how useful it would be if you knew more about the likes, dislikes, challenges, and preferences of your direct reports or team members. I recall a wise leader telling me, *We spend time getting to know people when we interview them for a job and then we seem to forget to ask any more questions and just expect them to perform and be satisfied.* To use a marriage analogy, the courtship ends once we've had the interview and we don't have to impress or find out any more about the other.

Marriage isn't such a far-flung analogy. Most of us spend

more time on the job than we do at home, so it follows that the quality of your work relationships influences the quality of your life. The quality of the relationship between a boss and direct report is regularly reported to be one of the most important factors in people's satisfaction at work. People often leave jobs or stay in jobs because of their boss. Consulting firm BlessingWhite's recent research on employee engagement found that "employees who know their managers 'very well' or 'well' trust them a lot more."[9]

At a minimum, you might know family members' names and any personal issues that might affect work, including health issues, death, or divorce. At the other end of the continuum, you might socialize together regularly. However, even knowing each other socially is no guarantee of a good working relationship or that socializing will facilitate business goals. The goal is to have enough of a relationship with people at work so each person feels respected and accepted as an individual. With such a relationship, you'll be in a much better position to delegate effectively, give feedback, assign stretch goals, and provide challenging assignments.

> The goal is to have enough of a relationship with people at work so each person feels respected and accepted as an individual.

Three elements necessary to building relationships.

1. DEVELOPING TRUST AND OPENNESS. All good relationships involve a level of trust and openness. Trust at work is defined[10] as a willingness to be vulnerable to another person because you believe there will be a positive outcome — meet a common goal, serve a greater good, deliver on promises — and that this person cares for and accepts you as an individual.

We can learn about building trust and openness from some interesting research about doctors who are sued compared with doctors who aren't.[11] The main finding indicated that patients were less likely to sue doctors who they felt cared about them

• • • **>** Every interaction

has the potential

to build closeness

or distance.

as individuals. This seemed to be the case even when a doctor was found to be actually at fault for malpractice. The doctors who were never sued spent more time with their patients, listened more actively, used humor, and made more 'positioning' comments like, *I'll examine you first, and then we'll have time to answer your questions.* These kinds of behaviors signal to patients that they are viewed as people, not just appointments.

Every interaction has the potential to build closeness or distance. Even direct reports and peers who work autonomously and who require minimal contact notice when their managers and team members spend little time with them or regularly postpone scheduled meetings for seemingly more important priorities. They also notice it when conversations are largely 'transactional.' Put yourself in the shoes of your employees or peers and imagine how you would feel if your conversations were limited to exchanges like *Can you do this?* and *We need to address that.* Ask yourself whether your last interaction with someone built closeness or distance in that relationship.

2. ADAPTING YOUR STYLE TO THE STYLE OF OTHERS.

Understanding differences in personal styles and not expecting others to conform to your own unique style can greatly enhance your work relationships. The most effective leaders adjust the words they use, what they emphasize, or what they expect from each individual based on their understanding of that person's style.

Knowing your own style and tendencies is critical in deciding whether to adapt the way you relate to others and how you might do that. If you understand your own style, you can more easily recognize the styles of others and learn to relate better. For example, some people respond best to details and facts, others to general concepts and the big picture. Knowing which way an individual is predisposed allows you to play to their strengths. An instrument called the MBTI™ describes some people as "Feelers" and others as "Thinkers." Feelers tend to prefer a stronger emphasis on personal relationships than do Thinkers.[12] That means they are more likely to be open to talking about feelings and values. In addition to the MBTI™, there are many other models and frameworks useful in identifying different styles and offering suggestions on how to effectively relate to each.[13]

3. UNDERSTANDING OTHERS. Finally, building relationships requires gaining an understanding of others, and this involves having quality conversations. In any conversation with a direct report or peer, you can alter the level of conversation based on the amount of openness and trust, and your personal preferences and style. To create appropriate conversations aimed at understanding others, it is helpful to have at your disposal a bank of questions I like to call Work Life questions.

The power of these kinds of conversations is supported by extensive research with married couples carried out by psychologist John Gottman.[14] He describes seven telltale signs of happy couples that stay married; he calls one of these signs Love Maps. Love Maps describe the degree to which couples know and understand each other. Gottman found that couples with happy marriages had a detailed understanding of each other's worlds: what they liked, their struggles, their backgrounds, concerns, and hopes. According to Gottman, Love Maps protected marriages when couples went through difficult periods.

Work Life conversations are a less intimate workplace version of this knowledge base. Work Life conversations create an opportunity to show respect for your direct reports, indicating that you care enough to want to get to know them as individuals. Research from the Gallup Organization strongly suggests that managers need to show employees that they care about them, that they want to help them develop and, more important, that they understand them.[15]

Work Life Questions

The following section is a bank of Work Life Questions for you to select from. You can also build on and modify the questions to suit your language and style of interacting. You can use Work Life questions in various ways. For example, you can ask employees to bring prepared answers to formal meetings, informal interactions over lunch or coffee (asking one or two each time you meet), or to team meetings. Asking peers, customers, and clients variations of the Work Life questions can effectively build those relationships as well. Making these kinds of conversations an ongoing part of your work relationships will help you, and those you work with, to understand each other's working style and how best to work together. The result is everyone will be more likely to want to give his or her best effort to the organization and be honest and direct with you.

Getting to know people's work style, strengths, and development areas:

1. What are your strengths?
2. How could you leverage your strengths even more?
3. If you used your strengths every day, what would you be doing differently?
4. What's the potential downside of your strengths?
5. What motivates you? What demotivates you?
6. What stresses you the most at work?
7. What do you feel most competent doing?
8. What skills do you need/want to develop?
9. What does a perfect working day look like for you?
10. In the last three months, what have you been most proud of accomplishing?
11. What would be the biggest compliment anyone could give you about your work? What's the best compliment you've ever received?
12. In the last three months, what have been your biggest challenges?
13. What obstacles or potential obstacles do you experience in your job?
14. What tasks do you enjoy most/least?

15. How do you best learn something new?

16. If you were working to your full potential, what would you be doing differently?

17. What have you learned lately — about yourself, your colleagues, or leadership?

Getting to know people's values and what's important to them:

18. What are three things that get you out of bed in the morning?

19. What is important to you — personally and professionally?

20. What kinds of situations at work get you mad/sad/glad?

21. In your career, what manager did you feel the most/least respect for and why?

22. Who do you admire the most in the organization and why?

23. What does success look like for you?

24. What would most likely cause you to leave the company?

25. Which aspects of work fit with and don't fit with your values?

26. What values are absolutely non-negotiable for you?

27. What do you most want to have an impact on?

28. If you were running this organization, what would you do first?

29. If you had another career, what would it be?

Relationships with others:

30. What do you think others (your peers, direct reports, superiors, customers, clients) would say about you if you could eavesdrop — about your strengths, development areas, and style?

31. What do you appreciate most about your team members?

32. Who do you get along with the most/least on the team? Why?

33. How much influence do you think you have with others (peers, superiors)?

34. How do you contribute positively/negatively to the team?

35. What role (rebel, challenger, mediator, good son/daughter) do you often take on the team?

36. How do you build trust in your working relationships?

37. How do you resolve conflicts or differences in your relationships?

Expectations between manager and direct report:

38. What do you expect from me as your manager?

39. What's your understanding of what I expect of you?

40. What would you like me to do more of/less of/the same of?

41. How can I support you in your job and in your development?

42. What do you appreciate/not appreciate about my leadership style?

43. How much personal conversation do you prefer?

44. How often would you like to have a meeting/contact with me?

45. How do you prefer to be given feedback?

46. How do you prefer to be delegated to (how much detail and autonomy, how often to check in on progress)?

47. What kind of information do you expect from me?

48. What else do you want me to know about how you operate?

49. If you were in my role, what would you do differently?

50. What's your understanding of what our priorities are?

51. How would you describe my working or leadership style to someone else?

Career aspirations and goals:

52. When you look over your work history, what role did you enjoy the most and why?

53. What do you consider your ideal job?

54. Where do you see yourself in a year/three to five years/ten years?

55. What is it about this career goal that you're interested in?

56. How ready do you think you are for the next step in your career?

57. What do you see as your next challenge?

58. What do you think you'll find the most challenging/rewarding aspect of your career goal?

59. How can I help you with your next career step?

BUILDING RELATIONSHIPS

❶ BE CLEAR ABOUT YOUR INTENTIONS. If you choose to use Work Life questions and people are not used to being asked about themselves, they may feel suspicious or uncomfortable. To create a safe environment, articulate your motivations and thoughts by initiating Work Life conversations saying, *I'd really like to find out more about you, how you're doing in your job, and what's important to you at this point in your life. Maybe we could start by talking about what is energizing you at work now.*

❷ DRAW WORK LIFE MAPS. Taking the concept of Work Life further, you can ask people to draw a picture or Work Life Map (a mind map[16]) on flipchart paper of the different aspects of their Work Life such as their team, other important relationships, main projects and personal information they want to include. This can generate a solid basis for useful conversations to build relationships and to explore aspects of peoples' work. Asking people to draw pictures of their work history is also another efficient and powerful way to understand and leverage others' experience and skills.

❸ KNOW PEOPLE'S CAREER GOALS. Have regular updates about the career aspirations of your direct reports and the steps they need to take to get there. Not everyone wants your job (or the CEO's), and it's important to respect people's goals even if they're not what you had in mind. People won't disclose what they want if they think you'll disapprove. Discussing career goals is also an important aspect of building relationships with your peers.

❹ MANAGING UPWARD: USE WORK LIFE QUESTIONS WITH YOUR MANAGER. You don't have to wait for your manager to initiate these conversations. Managing upward effectively involves taking proactive steps to ensure you and your manager develop a good working relationship. You could simply say, *I'd like us to understand more about how each other operates and how we can best work together.*

tips

Tool #2 focused on three elements: developing trust, adapting your style and understanding others.
These elements enhance your ability to build relationships and to understand how others think.
The next tool is designed to develop your ability to understand and work with less tangible factors that contribute to how we and others think, feel, behave and relate.

⑤ **VIRTUAL TEAMS: USE WORK LIFE QUESTIONS FOR TEAM BUILDING.** Work Life questions can be a very useful team-building tool for virtual teams that may not meet face-to-face very often. Try using one question a week as an icebreaker on a team call. It is a good idea to send it out in advance so people can think about it beforehand. Or, take turns spotlighting team members by asking them to answer a couple of questions so the team can get to know them better. If you are the team leader, be sure to take a turn. You could also ask team members to choose questions they would like to hear everyone's response to — they might make up some new and interesting ones.

⑥ **CROSS-CULTURAL TEAMS: MODIFY AND CREATE WORK LIFE QUESTIONS THAT FOCUS ON CROSS-CULTURAL UNDERSTANDING.** Most of the Work Life questions can be asked, as they are written or with slight modifications, in one-on-one conversations or during team meetings to highlight cultural influences. Here are some extra questions to consider in building understanding of different cultures: *What is the most important aspect of your culture that we/I need to understand? What do you see as the biggest difference between your culture and mine? What have you learned about working with someone from another culture that is important for the whole team to know?* Another slightly different and powerful question to ask people from another culture is how people from their culture would describe your culture.

 **Tool 3... Focus on Process**

A project team within a manufacturing company was having its regular weekly meeting. The meeting was running overtime, as usual, and there was still one important issue to discuss.

Andrew, a team member, had been speaking nonstop for the last ten minutes. He hadn't noticed that some people were checking their phones for messages while others looked bored and disengaged. Once Andrew starts talking about a topic he feels strongly about, it is hard to stop him.

After Andrew had finished speaking, the team leader, Pat, decided to rush through the last agenda item. She announced to the team that she would be bringing in a new team member to help with the workload, *I've been talking with Jeremy from Supply about his joining the team and he is happy to start next week.* Several people seemed pleased to hear this news and others sat quietly. Pat declared the meeting over and people filed out of the room.

As they walked out of the meeting together, Les said to Sally, *I think she's making a big mistake with Jeremy. He's not the right fit for this team.*

Sally agreed. *Not only that, but he is terrible to work with and he never does what he says he's going to do.*

Helen, another team member, overheard their conversation and confronted them. *Why didn't you two say something if you don't think it's a good idea? Pat should know about Jeremy if you don't think he should join the team.*

Les responded defensively. *What's the point? Pat does what she wants anyway. We're just team members so it doesn't matter what we think.*

> ● ● ● **>** These dynamics have organizational repercussions because, managed poorly, they can lead to wasted time, poor-quality decisions, lack of commitment to decisions, and low engagement levels.

You can probably relate to some aspects of this team-meeting scenario. Whether the interaction is with one other person or a group, these dynamics happen regularly: People dominate, discussions take too long, people disengage, and superficial decision-making processes prevent people from really committing to decisions. These dynamics have organizational repercussions because, managed poorly, they can lead to wasted time, poor-quality decisions, lack of commitment to decisions, and low engagement levels. Whether you are a team member or leader in a team meeting — or even if you are simply having a conversation with another person — you can influence dynamics in a way that can improve the quality of your conversations.

The Difference Between Task And Process

The first step in influencing the dynamics of interactions is to understand the difference between task and process. Knowing the difference will allow you to identify what is happening and what you can do to improve the interaction. Task is *what* you are talking about and working on; process refers to *how* you are talking or communicating about the task. Task includes the content, decisions, details, and facts. Process is more involved because it includes paying attention to the following:

On the surface:

- Participation levels
- Levels of understanding being expressed
- How decisions are being made or not being made
- What kind of interruptions occur, who dominates, who is ignored or talked over
- How disagreements or conflicting views are expressed and managed.

Below the surface:

- Energy and engagement levels
- People's feelings about issues
- People's judgments and feelings about others
- Unexpressed thoughts, hidden agendas, beliefs, motivations, and assumptions.

Most workplace conversations focus mainly on task. Process dynamics are usually not openly discussed even though they can have a significant impact on how an interaction evolves. Instead, people tend to avoid some meetings or conversations, manage around certain dynamics, or just accept unsatisfying interactions as a normal part of their working lives.

Balancing Focus Between Task And Process Is Critical

> Too much emphasis on the process can be at the expense of achieving the task.

Too much emphasis on the process can be at the expense of achieving the task. If you surface people's feelings and opinions on every issue, you risk hijacking the meeting. These discussions often go nowhere and there is little or no closure on important issues. On the other hand, too much focus on the task can mean that decisions are made too quickly without everyone's input and full participation. And when decisions are not fully discussed or thought through, people may have little or no buy-in.

Why Process Is Not Discussed

PROCESS CAN BE INVISIBLE OR HARD TO ARTICULATE. Task is easier to focus on because it is more tangible. Since process is not as obvious, we rarely talk about process dynamics like energy levels or a person's feelings or motivations. For example, it is rare to hear people say things like *I have noticed you seem tired. Would you like us to take a small break?* or *I have noticed people have had a strong reaction to this issue. I suggest we go around the table and hear from everyone.* It takes knowledge of process, courage, good leadership, and a climate of trust for these kinds of comments to be made — and heard and embraced.

WE HAVE A HABITUAL BIAS TOWARD TASK. Sometimes, a conversation is not flowing and no one knows exactly why. Even when people know why a conversation is not working, they may not know how to improve it. In either case, people tend to focus even more on the task than on the process. Have you ever repeated something for the sixth time, hoping that you would finally get through? Maybe you have found yourself asking more demanding questions of someone who is already defensive. Oftentimes, switching the focus to process can get you back on track. You can often recalibrate the conversation by asking questions or making comments like these: *I think we are approaching this issue with very different motivations. What is the most important factor for you?* and *Obviously, I do not understand what you're trying to tell me. What am I not getting?*

WE THINK IT WILL TAKE TOO MUCH TIME. Focusing on process can seem like an unproductive use of meeting time. There are usually too many issues and decisions to discuss as it is. However, investing some time in identifying process will actually save time in the end by improving the quality of decisions and ensuring constructive interactions between people. Imagine that a person who hasn't said a word in a meeting is specifically asked for her input. She raises a previously unmentioned crucial point that changes the course of a decision. Not only that, but the wider perception of the participants probably shifted when the process became more inclusive. In fact, research on 'fair process'[17] shows that when people feel their input is heard, they are more inclined to accept a decision even if they don't agree with it.

WE DON'T FEEL COMFORTABLE COMMENTING ON PROCESS. Many possible factors might make us reluctant to comment on process dynamics. We might work in an organizational culture where these kinds of conversations rarely happen, where there is strong pressure to stay on tasks only, or where strong hierarchical attitudes exist and managers control meetings and conversations. It can feel threatening to people to change focus from the task to dynamics. But if people understand why it is useful to talk about process, they are usually

● ● ● **>** However, investing some time in identifying process will actually save time in the end by improving the quality of decisions and ensuring constructive interactions between people.

more open to it. And it is often a relief for people to talk about the dynamics that are having a negative impact on a task or conversation.

How To Identify Process Dynamics

BOREDOM, CONFUSION, FRUSTRATION, DISTRACTION, AND DISENGAGEMENT. Any of these states can signal a need to reassess the situation. You can feel these emotions in relation to both task and process. The best way to tell if you need to focus on task or process is to ask yourself if you are having a reaction to *what* is being said or to *how* things are being discussed. For example, a colleague may be repeating himself, lecturing, or bringing up too many details but his point may be relevant. In this case, you might be having a reaction to *how* he is talking not to *what* he is saying.

RECURRING PATTERNS. An example of a recurring pattern is circular conversation where there is no closure. Another common recurring pattern could be that every time a particular person speaks, others interrupt or talk over him or her. Perhaps it's that someone becomes defensive, justifying, or arguing when asked questions.

What To Do When You Identify A Process Dynamic

A good general approach for confronting a process dynamic is to make an observation in a neutral way. Neutral language avoids 'loaded' words and phrases that negatively label others: *You're being arrogant* or *you don't know what you're talking about* are examples of loaded language. When intervening in a process dynamic, it's important to be as factual as possible without blaming or provoking strong reactions.

Author Bob Dick[18] suggests an escalating series of interventions for facilitating process dynamics.

- The first level of intervention involves making an observation. For example, in a group setting, an effective intervention might be *People are not really listening to each other.* Or, in a one-on-one conversation, *I think we are both trying to make our own points and are not listening to each other.*

- The second level of intervention involves making an observation, then making a suggestion and checking it out with others. In a group meeting, that intervention might sound like this: *I'm concerned that we've jumped straight into solution mode when I'm not sure we all understand the extent of the issue. I think it would be useful to find out more about the impact of this problem first. What do you think?* Or, in a one-on-one conversation, *I'm aware that you had some doubts about this idea. How do you feel about us discussing that now?*

Dick's framework works on this premise: The more process dynamics begin to hinder the task, the more people need structured suggestions of what to do. Structured suggestions might be as simple as suggesting you go around the table, asking each person what they think is really going on. Or, asking people to talk in pairs for a few minutes about what they think is *not* being said that is contributing to the dynamics. Learning how to facilitate process dynamics in this way is essential for leaders; it will help you run effective meetings, create buy-in, motivate and interest people, and ensure good quality decision making. In fact, these techniques are important for anyone in the workplace because we all take part in daily conversations and meetings that could be more productive.

FOCUSING ON PROCESS

❶ YOU DON'T NEED TO KNOW THE ANSWERS BEFORE YOU SAY SOMETHING. More important than having the answer is saying something that can pause a conversation long enough for people to stop and think about what is happening. In most cases, at least one other person will feel the same as you. To pause the conversation, try comments like: ***Does anyone else feel confused?*** Or ***I have no idea what's going on, but this conversation seems to be going in a circle. Does anyone have any ideas about what is going on?***

❷ WHEN IN DOUBT, SAY WHAT YOU'RE THINKING. People can often work out what to say simply by asking themselves, *What do I think is going on?* Sarah, a consultant colleague, complained to me about a frustrating project meeting with one of her clients that lasted two hours. She had tried to get her client to focus on the task, but her client kept taking the conversation in different directions. When I asked Sarah what she thought was going on, she said she thought her client was feeling concerned about the project — that his reputation was at stake and that he needed reassurance the project was on track. I asked her what would have happened if she had said exactly that. Without a moment's hesitation, she said the meeting would have been over in half an hour.

❸ OWN YOUR CONTRIBUTION TO THE DYNAMICS. Sometimes a process issue has more to do with us than anything else and we need to constantly monitor our own feelings and responses. During a conversation I might notice that the other person has become defensive. I may have been relating to this individual in an angry tone because of a different issue I have with this person (or because of a completely unrelated issue). My anger may be causing the defensiveness. I need to take responsibility for that and separate the issues. This can often be challenging to do in the middle of a heated conversation. One way to do this is to ensure that both sides slow down and understand the other person's perspective before reacting or 'counter-attacking.' Carl Rogers,[19] a pioneer of person-centered therapy whose influence is still relevant today, invented the technique of paraphrasing what a person says before continuing your side of an argument.

④ MANAGING UPWARD: TRUST YOUR INSTINCTS TO SPEAK UP. If you are feeling something is not quite right during a conversation, take a risk and say something. You can build a better relationship with your boss simply by saying *I don't quite understand the premise you're operating from. I'd like to understand it* or *I get the feeling you're not pleased with how I'm doing. Is that the case?*

⑤ VIRTUAL TEAMS: MANAGE PROCESS EXPLICITLY. High-performing virtual teams work proactively to manage process. They explicitly agree about how they will work together. For instance, a virtual team might define expectations about when a team member will return an instant message, email, or voice-mail. The team agrees on a code for requests that are 'urgent,' or 'need within 24 hours.' An effective virtual team will identify the important process guidelines critical to their work and spell out their expectations in areas such as decision making, regularity of communication, how to communicate, and how to divide tasks and review work. Using a facilitator who can debrief and encourage conversations about the team's process dynamics can be very helpful for virtual and cross-cultural teams.

⑥CROSS-CULTURAL TEAMS: DISCUSS CULTURAL EXPEC-TATIONS FOR BOTH TASK AND PROCESS. Many aspects of task and process vary according to different cultural dimensions. It is helpful to discuss and negotiate the expectations. For example, in relation to concepts of time, 'monochronic' cultures like the United States emphasize systematically working through agenda items, timely decisions and deadlines, and one person speaking at any one time. In contrast, 'polychronic' cultures like France are likely to experience strict agendas as limiting creativity, see deadlines as guidelines, and would be more used to several people talking at once.[20] Even simply asking at the beginning of meetings or conversations how a meeting like this would be conducted in the other person's culture can quickly highlight some cultural differences and similarities.

These are some of the ways to focus on process so that conversations and meetings might be more productive. A natural follow-up is recognizing and acknowledging emotions, a specific aspect of process dynamics, and our next tool in savvy leadership.

Tool 4…Recognize and Acknowledge Emotions

Jonathan, the finance director at a pharmaceutical company, rolled his eyes, took a deep breath, and braced himself as he spotted Peter, the sales director, heading toward him.

Here we go again, Jonathan said to himself as Peter entered his office. He had already had a very demanding day and didn't need Peter to add to it. Peter came straight to the point: *This is the second year in a row that bonuses have been late. We need to pay people when they expect us to.*

Jonathan responded firmly, *Look, I already told you that we'd get it sorted out soon. I've got more important priorities to deal with that you have no idea about.*

I appreciate that, but this is not the first time this has happened. People are starting to get cynical, and I shouldn't have to deal with them asking me every day. In an instant, Jonathan's face went bright red. He shouted at Peter, *Look, would you just leave me alone. I have other pressing issues.*

Peter abruptly left Jonathan's office, swearing under his breath. Jonathan shook his head, thinking that Peter was overreacting. He didn't realize the consequence of Peter's leaving their meeting feeling angry and disrespected. This was not the first time Peter had left an interaction with Jonathan feeling upset, but this incident was a turning point for him. The trust between them had been breached, and, as a result, their relationship was damaged. For the next month, Peter barely spoke to Jonathan and decided he would have as little to do with him as possible. Jonathan's inability to recognize and acknowledge the emotions that Peter and his sales team were feeling about their late bonuses had propelled a standoff.

Apart from the damage to their working relationship, Peter's decision had several organizational consequences. During executive team meetings, the tension between Peter and Jonathan created an uneasy atmosphere. Peter openly disagreed with Jonathan's comments. Some directors began to take sides depending on whom they were closer to. Discussions became unfocused. Decisions took longer. Employees began to comment about the executive team's lack of cohesion and this affected morale. Their direct reports also noticed their uneasy relationship and spent time gossiping about it. While direct reports waited for decisions that required the cooperation and agreement of Peter and Jonathan, even more time was wasted.

The Importance Of Recognizing And Acknowledging People's Emotions

Recognizing emotions is a foundational skill of being emotionally intelligent. Emotional intelligence is the ability to recognize, facilitate, understand, and manage emotions in yourself and others.[21] Recognizing and then acknowledging people's emotions affects how people feel during and after their interaction with you — and how well people will cooperate with you in the future. It can also make interactions more efficient. When emotions are not acknowledged, people tend to keep bringing them up in some way until they are. Emotional intelligence research shows that if people are feeling negative, they are more likely to think negatively and focus on details and errors. If you help them to feel differently, you can also influence them to think in a more creative way.[22]

> **>** When emotions are not acknowledged, people tend to keep bringing them up in some way until they are.

People are often not aware that they are feeling negative or dissatisfied and that these emotions are influencing the way they think. Without realizing it, they can end up sabotaging or undermining a discussion by continually raising issues and sources of dissatisfaction. Does this sound familiar? In our intimate relationships, how often do our partners want us to understand how they're feeling and not try to convince them they shouldn't have those feelings? We make the common mistake of trying to fix the problem, and the conversation ends up going around in circles or in conflict — or both. As author Nancy Kline[23] has noted, we stop thinking when we're upset; when we've expressed our feelings enough, we can start thinking again.

How Could Jonathan Have Responded Differently?

Let's look again at Peter and Jonathan's conversation and see what might have happened had Jonathan acknowledged the emotions this situation evoked.

Peter starts in the same way: *This is the second year in a row that bonuses have been late. We need to pay people when they expect us to.*

This time, Jonathan responds differently: *I'm guessing that people are feeling frustrated and angry. If I were in your place, I'd feel annoyed to have to deal with their emotions when it's something you have no control over. Have I got that right?*

Peter: *Yes, that's exactly right. I really don't know what to say anymore without sounding like I'm blaming your team. It comes up every day.*

Jonathan: *I'm sorry but you are probably going to have to manage this a bit longer and I know you won't be happy about that. Given that it's going to take a few more weeks, what do you suggest we do?*

Peter: *Well, maybe you can talk to the team in person and give them a specific idea of when they'll get their bonuses.*

Jonathan: *That's a good idea. Let's schedule the meeting.*

This time, Peter walked away feeling his relationship with Jonathan had been enhanced and they now had a strategy. Acknowledging the emotions in many situations can bring unexpected and satisfying results. It doesn't have to take a lot of effort on your part and can have a big impact on how positive or negative the other person feels toward you. It encourages people to tell you what they are really thinking about, oftentimes opening your eyes to issues you need to be aware of. Acknowledging emotions can also minimize the risk of unproductive conflict. Although we know emotions play a large part in our lives, we habitually tend to avoid talking about them. Multiple factors contribute to this avoidance.

> ● ● ● **(>)** Feelings are not up for negotiation or debate — people feel what they feel and the sooner they feel acknowledged, the sooner they can engage in the next phase of a conversation.

Why We Overlook People's Emotions

WE THINK IT WILL TAKE TOO LONG. Many people think that talking about emotions will veer a conversation off the issue. You can still talk about someone's emotions and stay on the task. In fact, acknowledging emotions can focus on people's real concerns faster. You can resolve their issues then and there, rather than having to circle back later. Often, all it takes is one statement for another person to feel their emotions have been acknowledged. Try an acknowledgement like this: *I can hear that you're struggling with this project. What are your biggest challenges?*

WE THINK THINGS WILL GET OUT OF CONTROL AND WE WON'T KNOW WHAT TO DO. There is often a fear that the person will become more emotional if you acknowledge their feelings. In fact, people are more likely to get out of control if you don't validate their feelings. The best thing you can do is give people the opportunity to say what they're feeling without trying to control things. When upset people are allowed to vent their emotions, they are usually able to move on in the discussion. You don't have to do anything else.

If the situation does feel like it is getting out of control, try to relax, keep breathing, and acknowledge the person's feelings. Try to steer the individual toward a logical conversation. You might say *Obviously, you've been upset about this for a very long time. Tell me your main concerns.* Write down the issues with the intention of going through them one at a time after they have been recorded. If the person is unable to have a rational conversation, continue acknowledging their feelings. Then you might say *I can see this is a very emotional issue for you. Maybe we can reschedule this meeting and talk more about your concerns when you feel ready. What do you think?*

WE DON'T WANT PEOPLE TO CONCLUDE THAT WE AGREE WITH THEM. Acknowledging someone's feelings is not the same as agreeing with what they feel. All you are doing is saying that you can see that the person is feeling a certain way in relation to an event. Feelings are not up for negotiation or debate — people feel what they feel and the sooner they feel acknowledged, the sooner they can engage in the next phase of a conversation.

WE THINK WE MIGHT BE WRONG. Sometimes we have a sense that someone feels strongly about a situation, but we feel awkward about bringing it up in case we are wrong and unsure of what to say next. A safe way to raise the topic of someone's feelings is to ask *How do you feel about this?* In some cases, this is not enough; especially if someone tells you they're fine when you are convinced they're not.

In general, it helps to put yourself in another person's shoes. Their posture, facial expressions, gestures, and tone of voice can help you read their nonverbal communication.[24] If you can't read them but have a suspicion about how they might be feeling, say something in a way that leaves room for the person to agree or disagree. For example, *I'm not sure if I'm completely off track here. I have a feeling that maybe you weren't too happy in that meeting.* If you're wrong, they'll either tell you what they were feeling or deny it. Even if they deny it, you may have helped them let go of their feelings and get closer to moving on. If you get it completely wrong, that's okay; at least you've shown that you're interested in their feelings. Simply say, *Sorry, I got it wrong. I must have misread what I thought was going on with you.*

IT'S JUST HARD TO DISCUSS EMOTIONS. You're not alone if you feel uncomfortable talking about emotions. This is very common for people who are used to dealing with logic, facts, and data. In some ways, it is a habit that can be changed by being more aware of your own emotions and by learning and practicing the following coaching tips.

RECOGNIZING AND ACKNOWLEDGING EMOTIONS

❶ REMEMBER THAT EMOTIONS ARE INFORMATION.

Your feelings and other's feelings are important data that need to be factored into your thinking along with other data. You may register a feeling of unease when a particular issue is being talked about and this might lead you to focus more intently on why you might be feeling this way. Knowing how you or others feel may not change your intended actions but can certainly inform how you implement or communicate decisions. For example, if you know people are going to have negative reactions in relation to your meeting's first agenda item, you may consider moving that topic to a later time in the meeting.

❷ A GOOD FORMULA IS *ACKNOWLEDGE, THEN ASK.*

Acknowledge the emotion and then ask an open question that starts with *what, how, when.* Or encourage the other person by starting a sentence with *Tell me more ...* or *I'd like to know ... .* An example of an acknowledgement followed by an open question might go like this: *If I hear you right, you are disappointed that you didn't get that position. Tell me more about your disappointment.* Other ways to phrase acknowledgment of emotions include: *It seems ... , I get the feeling ... , You feel ... , I see you are feeling ... , I wonder if you're feeling ... , That must be frustrating... .*

Depending on the answer, you can either probe further or move the conversation along. If the person displays strong emotions, you will probably need to continue to acknowledge and explore. If their emotions are not strong, acknowledge them and then move toward action sooner: *As I understand it, you're disappointed that you didn't get that position. How do you feel about staying in your current role?*

tips

❸ MATCH YOUR 'FEELING' WORD TO THE INTENSITY OF THE PERSON'S FEELINGS. If someone is furious about a situation, your saying *You seem a little annoyed* will make him or her even angrier. Try to use words that are commensurate with the emotions: ***It seems to me that you're extremely angry with this and want something done about it immediately. Is that right?*** Similarly, when someone feels strongly, saying *I understand* or *I see* doesn't show people that you understand or see what they're feeling at all. It could appear that you're understating what they're feeling or only going through the motions of being empathic.

❹ USE 'UNLOADED' WORDS. Loaded words such as *stressed, defensive*, and *impatient* usually have a negative connotation and sound judgmental. Sometimes we don't realize a word is loaded for a particular person until they react negatively to what we've said. Some words may be loaded for some people and not for others. Try to find a positive aspect of the person's behavior. Compare saying something like ***You're concerned about your team's performance*** versus *You're controlling your team* or ***You're very committed to being efficient*** versus *You're micromanaging!* Remember that your tone of voice will also have a significant impact on how your message is interpreted even if your words are neutral or positive.

❺ MANAGING UPWARD: ACKNOWLEDGE YOUR BOSS'S FEELINGS AND TELL HIM HOW YOU FEEL. Don't assume that your manager is emotionally intelligent and manages his feelings so well that there's no need to discuss them. In fact, many managers try to protect their direct reports from what they are feeling and believe that no one has noticed. By acknowledging your boss's feelings, you may help to clarify issues. Letting him know that his feelings have been noticed may well enhance your relationship. In addition, telling your manager how his behavior affects you can be powerful — and rare — feedback. Imagine the potential impact of this candid admission: ***When you cancel our meetings more than twice, I feel unimportant and low priority and tend to want to give you less information about what I'm doing.***

⑥ VIRTUAL TEAMS: STRATEGICALLY MANAGE EMOTIONS AND RELATIONSHIPS. Research has shown that teams that are able to develop trust quickly, demonstrate enthusiasm, optimistic attitudes, and initiative, which then result in increased levels of collaboration.[25] Many authors suggest that virtual teams should have a one- or two-day workshop when they initially form to accelerate the process of building solid working relationships and trust. Given that members of virtual teams don't often meet face-to-face, even with an initial team-building event there is a high risk of misunderstandings and trust not being maintained. Having guidelines about when face-to-face meetings or computer-mediated meetings should take place, such as when there are conflicts, sensitive or emotional issues, or complicated negotiations can help to manage emotions and relationships in an ongoing way.[26]

⑦ CROSS-CULTURAL TEAMS: ASK COLLEAGUES ABOUT THEIR CULTURES' ATTITUDES TOWARD EMOTIONS. Research shows that there is universal agreement in recognizing many human emotions like sadness, anger, and happiness.[27] However, the norms or display rules regarding the *expression* of emotions differ from one culture to another. Even though it may still be helpful to acknowledge people's emotions, some people may not be comfortable having their feelings made public. Cultures can also differ in how much they separate their emotions from work issues. For example, cultures like The Netherlands and Sweden are less likely to show emotions and may view emotional expression in the workplace as

tips

unprofessional. Since they tend to separate their emotions from the issue, they may seek a more indirect response that supports their reasoning or thinking. Italians and Southern Europeans are more likely to show their emotions and may seek direct responses to them as part of the issues being discussed.[28] Taking a respectful and inquiring approach to how emotions are expressed and people's expectations of how their emotions will be responded to will help to reduce potential misunderstandings or people feeling insulted or embarrassed.

Having discussed the need to identify and manage emotions and more complex dynamics during conversations, we're ready to look at how you can be even more 'hands-on' to ensure you achieve the best outcomes from your interactions. The next tool explores the critical need to make time to think about and plan for your conversations.

⚙ Tool 5... Prepare for Conversations

When coaching clients on planning and interacting strategically, I often find it helpful to ask them to write verbatim accounts of their important conversations.

First, we read the document together as if we were reading a play, and then we analyze each sentence. This exercise allows clients to see the words they use more clearly, to understand the impact these have on others and what feelings arose during the discussion. Once they have had practice in writing and reviewing their 'verbatims' they begin to see where their conversations go off track.

The following is a small section from the beginning of a performance management discussion that a manager had with her direct report. At the end of each sentence in her verbatim, the manager also wrote the feelings she experienced and what she believed her direct report felt during their conversation.

Manager: *I wanted to talk to you about the fact that you are taking personal calls all the time. (Slightly annoyed)*

Employee: *No, I don't! (Defensive)*

Manager: *You always seem to be talking to a friend or someone personal. (Angry)*

Employee: *I do not. Like everyone else, I make private calls but not all the time. (Angry)*

Manager: *Okay, not all the time, but a lot of the time. (Trying to calm down)*

Employee: *I do my work and I get results, so what's the problem? (Stubborn)*

Manager: *I'm not saying you don't get good results — I am talking about making personal phone calls. (Frustrated)*

At this early stage of the discussion, the manager has already lost focus on what she wanted to address and now has to engage with someone who has become defensive. In retrospect, this manager realized that she needed to give more thought about what she was going to say and how her direct report might respond.

 • • • **>** Every conversation we have has a positive, negative, or neutral impact on our relationships.

Preparing For Conversations

Every conversation we have has a positive, negative, or neutral impact on our relationships. Susan Scott says in her book, *Fierce Conversations*[29] "the conversation is the relationship." Given that the quality of our relationships is influenced by each conversation we have, it is helpful to prepare for them, whenever possible. Most of us prepare for the content of a conversation with numbers, tables, graphs, facts, data, and evidence. We are less likely to plan the words we will use, and far less likely to prepare for the emotional aspects of our conversations.

As in the scenario of the personal phone calls, we have all experienced a conversation in which we sense we've just said the wrong thing and feel we may as well pack up and go home. The conversation seems almost impossible to retrieve as it spirals off in a direction we didn't intend. We can't control how someone else will react during a conversation, but we can prepare in ways that will maximize the possibility of making conversations more constructive and positive.

If we don't take the time to think about the situation we are about to discuss and the words we will use, there is a higher risk that the conversation will go off course. For a conversation that is likely to be difficult, it's particularly critical to plan — and rehearse — what you will say. Let's look at some classic aspects of communication that can potentially throw a conversation off course. Fortunately, by thinking about and preparing for these potentialities, you can manage conversations to better effect.

Conversation Showstoppers

SWEEPING STATEMENTS AND GENERALIZATIONS. Saying things like *all the time*, *always*, and *never* is like waving a red flag in front of a bull. The other person gets hooked by these kinds of words and then argues about them, rather than focusing on the actual issue. In the scenario of the personal phone calls, it would have been better to have planned to say ***up to three personal phone calls a day.***

NEGATIVE NONVERBAL COMMUNICATION. People respond to many aspects of nonverbal communication, including the tone of your voice, your facial expressions, your hand and body gestures, and the attitude behind what you say. Many theorists suggest that nonverbal communication accounts for between 60 and 93 percent of what we say.[30] Even if you're using neutral language but have an attitude of accusation or judgment, people will most likely respond to your attitude.

LOADED WORDS. I recall a team member trying to calm someone down during a meeting by telling her she was being a martyr. As soon as that word was used, the discussion instantly heated up and the team had to go into damage control quickly. Words like *should* and *must* can evoke a defensive response in others.

TOO MANY 'YOU' STATEMENTS. Overusing the words *you* and *your* creates defensive attitudes in others. The perceived accusation has the effect of disengaging people from further productive participation in the conversation. In the scenario of the personal phone calls, *you always seem to be ... and you are taking ...* are examples of 'you' statements. Try using 'I' when- ever appropriate to balance things out: ***I'm concerned about the number of personal calls you're making.***

AVOIDING TAKING RESPONSIBILITY. One of the main reasons people use '*you*' instead of '*I*' is because they don't — or won't — see that they've contributed to what has happened. Though this is true in some cases, there are many times when we are at least partly responsible for outcomes. For example, Bill complained about his manager's response to his ongoing requests for more time together. Bill had told his manager that she didn't make enough time for them to discuss work and that he had attempted to ensure they met, without success. She responded by telling him that that was his problem. That was as far as their last interaction went. Consider what might have happened instead if the manager had responded by taking some responsibility for their lack of communication: ***I can see*** ***how my schedule has also made it very difficult for us to find time to meet.*** Taking some responsibility for your part in a situation can lead to both parties being in a better position to negotiate a mutual solution and minimizes the chance of anyone taking a 'victim' position.

Preparing For The Emotional Side Of Discussions

Being able to recognize and acknowledge emotions helps you engage with emotions that surface during interactions. You are more likely to be able to manage people's emotions if you anticipate them. Obviously, emotions that we haven't expected will arise. However, there are many scenarios where we can predict people's feelings before we meet with them.

Tom was about to have a challenging meeting with one of his direct reports who didn't get a position she had applied for. He had spent time thinking about how to make her current job more interesting so he could make up for her inevitable disappointment. Tom was also planning to tell her about another position in a different part of the business that he thought would interest her. Although she would probably have welcomed Tom's plans eventually, he hadn't given much thought to how his direct report might feel during the conversation. When asked what he thought about what she might be feeling, Tom had no trouble coming up with a list: anger, disappointment, frustration, and confusion about why she hadn't gotten the position. Once Tom began to think about the emotional side of the discussion, he could plan the meeting a little differently. To start with, at the beginning of the meeting he would give her time and 'permission' to express her feelings about missing out on the job she wanted. By thinking ahead of time about how you will say certain things and what emotions might be present, you can prepare more strategically for conversations.

> One of the main reasons people use 'you' instead of 'I' is because they don't — or won't — see that they've contributed to what has happened.

PREPARING FOR CONVERSATIONS

❶ PLAN THE PURPOSE, TIME AND LOCATION OF YOUR MEETING. Think about the purpose of your meeting and what you want to convey. If you want to create an open and honest environment, sitting behind your desk is not the ideal position. Would a local cafe´or a conference room be more appropriate than your office? Consider what else might be happening in any given week before setting the date and time of your meeting. Plan on stating the purpose of meeting at the outset, even if you think it's already been said before. Barbara Minto, the author of an informative book on how to structure messages we want to get across, suggests that if people have to use limited energy to guess what you're talking about, they have less energy to focus on the important messages you want to give.[31] It is also very helpful to ask others what they would like to discuss.

❷ THINK ABOUT YOUR LANGUAGE. Rehearsing or writing down the sentences or words you want to use can make a significant difference in your conversations. Edit out general-izations, loaded words, and superfluous 'you' statements. With some forethought, you might control an impulse to say *You're never going to reach any of your targets if you keep going the way you're going* and replace it with a more productive ***I'm concerned about whether you'll be able to reach your targets for this month.***

❸ THINK ABOUT YOUR EMOTIONS. It is useful to think about what kind of mood you'd like to be in for your conversations or meetings. We often accept whatever mood we're in without realizing that we can change our mood more than we think. In the phone call scenario, the manager's annoyed tone at the beginning of the meeting contributed to how the conversation evolved. Emotional intelligence research teaches us that we can change our moods to suit the situation. For example, if you're in a negative mood (and therefore might be more fault-finding than normal) it might be best to reschedule an important meeting you're about to have or go for a brisk walk to shift how you're feeling. Writing feelings and thoughts down (journaling) and physical exercise are two proven techniques for changing mood states.[32]

❹ RETRIEVE A CONVERSATION. Until someone has walked out — and even then, the conversation isn't over and can be salvaged — there's a chance to rescue a negative conversation. If a conversation 'goes south,' apologize if appropriate to get a conversation back on track and to give the other person an opportunity to express what they're thinking and feeling. Apologetic language might not come naturally. Plan to say any of the following or your own variation, if the need arises. *I'm sorry. I've said things in a way I didn't intend. Can we start again?* Or *I don't think this meeting is going very well. What is upsetting you?* Or *you seem concerned about what I've just said. Tell me what's on your mind.*

❺ MANAGING UPWARD: PREPARE THOROUGHLY AND VISIBLY. Most managers appreciate their direct reports' coming to meetings with notes that list questions, important points, and ideas. Even if you're only discussing something casually, the fact that you have prepared in advance can save time, enhance the conversation, and make an impression on your manager.

❻ VIRTUAL TEAMS: HAVE PREPARED GUIDELINES FOR MEETINGS AND CONVERSATIONS. Ensuring that videoconference or phone meetings are productive involves defining procedures that will take place. For example, at the beginning of a meeting, introduce each person so everyone knows who's on the call; send the agenda in advance, and start and finish on time. For decision making, use a 'propose and poll' process. Once a proposed decision is articulated, each person responds with either yes or no. Then, each person who said no is asked to elaborate about his or her views. After more discussion, another poll is taken. This process may continue for several rounds before a decision is reached.[33]

tips

❼ CROSS-CULTURAL TEAMS: PLAN CAREFULLY FOR CULTURAL NORMS. A range of cultural differences affects conversations. Certain cultures with formal and rigid hierarchy require that the participants in a conversation be of the same or similar status. Position and age may need to be equal to show respect. In some cultures, an intermediary is brought in to 'translate' between two very different cultural approaches. It is also important to understand if the other culture is 'individual-istic' (like the US, Australia, Great Britain, Canada) or 'collectivistic' (such as Colombia, Pakistan, Indonesia, South Korea).[34] In an individualistic culture, feedback delivered to an individual is considered to pertain to that individual alone. But in a collectivistic culture, feedback to an individual is assumed feedback to the entire group. Planning for how you will address people is also very important. Some cultures view titles as a sign of status and if a leader's status is downgraded, all their subordinates are downgraded as well.[35]

Getting into the habit of preparing for conversations pays off in more productive communication and a greater probability of achieving desired outcomes. The next tool *Ask, Don't Tell* will further strengthen your technique in interpersonal interactions.

⚙ Tool 6...Ask, Don't Tell

For what seemed like the hundredth time, James had just finished telling his direct report Julie to deal with a team member who wasn't doing his job properly.

James, frustrated with having to say the same thing repeatedly, said he couldn't understand what the problem was. Julie seemed uninterested and James felt she wasn't taking her role as a manager seriously. Furthermore, James was tired of doing parts of Julie's job. He didn't know what to do next, so he contacted me for some coaching sessions.

At our first session, I asked James what he wanted to achieve. He had recently been promoted to a senior role in which several managers reported to him.

He wasn't happy with his team's performance and was at a loss as to what to do about it. His boss had told him he needed to lead his people rather than manage them as he had in previous roles. James agreed with his boss: he needed to be more of a leader. I asked him what he meant.

> **Telling does have its place. But if it's your style of choice and you don't have other approaches in your toolbox, it can be counterproductive in the longer term.**

Well, I have to motivate my managers so they can get their teams to achieve their objectives, he said. *But I tend to be a bit aggressive sometimes.*

I asked what he meant by aggressive. I admired James' honesty and insight and felt I needed to get to the bottom of what he thought he needed to change.

I know I probably don't give them much of a chance to talk. I tend to tell them what I want done.

So James, when you have a conversation with one of your staff, what percentage of the time do you talk and how much do they talk?

James took a moment before he replied that it was probably a ratio of 80/20.

You mean 80 percent you and 20 percent them?

James nodded and looked a little surprised. We sat in silence for a moment contemplating what he had just said.

The Case For 'Telling'

James' approach to leading his people is not uncommon. He needed to get results and thought the best way to do that was to tell people what to do and it seemed to work in his previous positions. James' management style reminded me of something another senior leader once said about his 'telling' style: *That's what I'm paid to do, isn't it? That's why I was hired for this job. I have the experience and am expected to come up with answers.* Telling is what managers have done since managers first existed. There are several reasons why this is still a popular way to lead people.

IT'S QUICK. You can immediately give people all the information you need them to have. And you don't spend time trying to get them to work it out when you're in a hurry and you already have a good solution to a problem.

YOU FEEL YOUR EXPERIENCE IS PUT TO USE. All those years of experience that you've clocked up can be passed onto your staff. This means they don't have to reinvent the wheel or risk doing an inferior job.

IT WORKS WELL UNDER CERTAIN CONDITIONS. Telling is the essence of a directive leadership style. A directive style is best suited to short-term situations when people don't have the required skills or lack motivation. It can also be effective in a crisis.

Telling does have its place. But if it's your style of choice and you don't have other approaches in your toolbox, it can be counterproductive in the longer term. Let's consider James again. He admitted that his style wasn't working. His direct reports were not doing what he wanted and he wasn't happy with how they were managing their teams. When I asked James about the pros and cons of the telling style, he easily added points to the downside.

Downside Of Telling

PEOPLE STOP THINKING FOR THEMSELVES. When we tell people what to do or think, they actually don't have to think because we've done it for them. Doing this regularly can set up a pattern where people start to expect us to solve even simple problems because they're not used to having to think for themselves. Many leaders complain about their staff not thinking creatively or innovatively enough; if this is your situation, ask yourself if you are giving your staff a chance to do otherwise.

PEOPLE ARE LESS LIKELY TO TAKE RESPONSIBILITY. People are most likely to take responsibility for a task or project when they have been involved in thinking about it or solving it.

You've probably had at least one experience in the workplace when you've asked someone to do something more than once knowing that even though they said they would, they wouldn't. Did this person feel any responsibility for the project or task at hand? Telling them what to do practically guarantees they will remain unengaged.

YOU MISS OPPORTUNITIES TO DEVELOP PEOPLE. Habitually telling people what to do sets up a vicious cycle: You tell them what to do, and the more you tell them, the more they don't develop their own skills and expertise. You also sabotage a critical aspect of your own role as a leader, which is to develop people. It's hard to attract and retain good people if your company has a reputation for not focusing on developing people.

YOU CAN BE SEEN AS INTIMIDATING OR PATRONIZING. Telling people what to do can be perceived as being bossy, demeaning, or just plain annoying. If telling is an ingrained habit in your leadership style, chances are you might not be aware of how you affect people. Your direct reports or peers most likely have noticed; however, they may have decided not to tell you how it affects them. A telling style discourages honest feedback.

YOU DON'T APPEAR TO BE INTERESTED IN OTHERS. Even if you say you are interested in people's opinions or viewpoints, your actions are what count. If you don't ask questions, people might think you are not interested in their perspective. Telling just makes it even more obvious to others that you're not really interested in a two-way exchange or a real relationship.

The impact of a habitual telling style can be significant. Sometimes, people will seem to be going along with you but will undermine your decisions and end up doing their own thing. You run the risk of creating a reputation as a leader or peer who people don't respect and don't want to work with. People who work in a telling environment may feel demoralized, going through the motions while waiting for a better job elsewhere. They do not feel trusted to think for themselves. In a situation like this, you can end up creating the very culture you don't want: people who don't think for themselves or take responsibility for getting results.

Asking Questions Is A Powerful Antidote To Telling

As James discovered, the simplest way to reverse your telling/listening ratio is to ask more questions and really listen to the answers. He came back to his second session in a good mood. He had practiced asking more questions and found his direct reports starting to take their roles as managers more seriously. He thought he still had a long way to go but felt optimistic about his ability to tell less and trust that his managers could do their jobs effectively. Most managers change their telling/listening ratio quickly once they realize what they're doing, and they end up satisfied with the results. A senior manager once said to me: *This is like magic; I used to end up with 10 things on my to-do list. This 'not telling' stuff really works. I don't have a thing on my list after that meeting with my direct report.*

 As James discovered, the simplest way to reverse your telling/listening ratio is to ask more questions and really listen to the answers.

ASKING, NOT TELLING

❶ ASK OPEN-ENDED QUESTIONS. Open questions encourage people to take responsibility and think for themselves. Start your sentences with *what, when,* and *how.* Questions like *How have you begun resolving this problem so far?* and *What do you think should be the first steps in planning this project?* invite participation and encourage responsibility and involvement.

❷ MINIMIZE CLOSED QUESTIONS. Closed questions save time and can usually be answered with a *yes, no,* or other brief response. Sometimes they can efficiently go to the core of an issue like *Do you trust me?* or *How long has this been a problem? However, Did you try calling the customer back?* is a closed question with an implication about what the person should have done. Many closed questions start with:

Didn't you … Shouldn't you … Can't you … Couldn't you … Did you …

They tend to tell people what to do in an indirect manner and do not enhance relationships.

❸ AIM FOR A 20/80 BALANCE: 20 percent you talking, 80 percent your direct report or peer talking — in most of your conversations. This is only a guide. Obviously, there will be some discussions in which it's totally appropriate for you to give information — say, when you are explaining a new procedure or setting expectations. Even in these kinds of conversations, you can incorporate questions. Set an inclusive tone by asking *What has been your approach to doing this in previous jobs?* or *How would you like us to work together in this area?*

❹ BE OPEN TO NEW THOUGHTS AND IDEAS. Even open questions can close down a conversation if asked when you already have the answer and are steering the person to say exactly that. *What have I told you before about resolving this kind of problem?* leads nowhere. ***What are the possible options***

for resolving this kind of problem? might well lead to an idea or approach you had not considered. Try asking questions with a spirit of genuine inquiry or exploration. You might be surprised by others' ideas.

⑤ MANAGING UPWARD: AVOID 'WHY' QUESTIONS. Questions starting with *why* tend to sound blaming and can encourage others to look for excuses or rationalizations. *Why* questions can also provoke a defensive reaction, especially if you are dealing with a manager who may not be used to being asked questions by a direct report. Consider the difference between asking *Why did you do that?* and saying ***I'd like to understand more about how you came to that decision.***

⑥VIRTUAL TEAMS: MAKE THE EFFORT TO ASK. The point of virtual teams is to have the best talent possible despite location, so by definition, everyone has something to contribute. But when communication is mainly by phone and email, taking the time to ask for everyone's opinion has to be a deliberate choice. Build in time to go around the team asking each person's opinion, or use software that allows team members to enter their ideas in a file for all members to review.

⑦ CROSS-CULTURAL TEAMS: EXPLORE WHAT PEOPLE REALLY MEAN WHEN THEY ANSWER QUESTIONS. In some cultures, a *yes* response to your question may only mean the person is listening, or it may mean *maybe*. In cultures where power and hierarchy are highly defined, people may be uncomfortable answering questions, especially when someone who is considered a superior is in the room. Some people may prefer to answer questions in ways that minimize conflict rather than risk damaging relationships. People from collectivist cultures prefer to maintain harmony and avoid direct confrontation compared to people from individualist cultures where speaking

directly about what one thinks is seen as being honest.[36] In asking questions of people who may be indirect, it can be helpful to probe with gentle, follow-up questions that pick-up on words they use to ensure you get to the essence of what they are not able to say. For example, ***What do you mean when you say that the situation is okay?*** or ***If it was better than okay, what would it be like?*** Maintaining a non-judgmental attitude is also essential.

Using these tips will help you to strategically and tactically handle the direction of your conversations. The final two tools are particularly designed to assist you to create a foundation in your workplace where powerful conversations are the norm. *Explore Before Problem Solving* is the first of these tools.

Tool 7... Explore Before Problem Solving

This anecdote illustrates that people don't always want or expect a solution or explanation when they raise issues.

A colleague came into my office and started complaining about how busy he was, how problematic his project was, and how difficult his client was. He seemed troubled and obviously needed help — or so I thought. Once he'd finished telling me all his woes, I prepared to tell him what I thought he should do based on my experience. Before I even managed to say a word, he suddenly said, *I feel better now, thanks for that.* And off he went to continue his work in his usual efficient manner.

• • • **>** When we're

functioning as

if everything is a

crisis, everything

becomes a crisis.

Sometimes people just want to think out loud, express their feelings, or just be listened to. They may want to work something out for themselves with your input. In other instances, people do want you to help them with solutions. If you go into problem solving prematurely, you miss the real issue or focus on the wrong issue. More important, you don't allow the opportunity for the person to figure something out for himself or herself. A veteran trainer I've worked with often used to say, *Every time you solve something for someone or tell him or her what to think, you risk disempowering him or her.* Why do we so easily and habitually go into explaining or 'fix it' mode?

Why We're Tempted To Fix Problems

WE EMPHASIZE SPEED. The more advanced our technology, the more pressure to respond to requests and emails immediately, even on holidays. Many organizations emphasize getting things done quickly and using time productively. Fixing a problem fast feels like an accomplishment.

WE OFTEN CREATE THE CRISIS. Because of our emphasis on speed, we often find ourselves operating in high gear. When we're functioning as if everything is a crisis, everything becomes a crisis. In this mode, we're more likely to feel impatient with discussion or analysis, preferring immediate solutions and actions.

PROBLEM SOLVING IS HABITUAL. We tend to default to problem solving. If we tell someone about a problem, they usually try to fix it. In many cases, this is an expected response and is what most managers and knowledge workers believe they are paid to do.

EMOTIONS CAN BE UNCOMFORTABLE. Sometimes, we want to solve people's problems because we feel uncomfortable with their struggle or discomfort. We may not even realize when we steer conversations in directions that make us feel more comfortable.

WE WANT TO FEEL COMPETENT. Knowing the answers makes us feel comfortable and competent. Helping others gives us a positive feeling and makes us feel on top of things. Some solutions can be so obvious that we would feel almost negligent if we didn't respond. It's not surprising that many managers have had to learn that it's okay to say *I don't know the answer to that. Let's think about it.*

Quickly responding to and solving issues, challenges, and problems is often the best response. But there are instances when pausing for a moment, asking further questions, and checking what kind of response is expected or desired can be even better. Exploring a situation thoroughly before problem solving can ensure you address the right issue. Making this more thoughtful approach a habit can enhance your work relationships.

Traps Of Premature Problem Solving

WE ASSUME WORDS HAVE THE SAME MEANING TO EVERYONE. It is amazing how often we use words like *communication* and *leadership* and assume everyone else defines them the same way. Even a simple word like *fun* can mean something different to each of us. During a team-building workshop a team member complained that the team didn't have enough fun together. Just as the team leader was about to ask for the team's agreement to organize a dinner, I asked the team what fun meant to them. Every person had a different meaning. By the time we'd heard from everyone, it was clear a team dinner was not the best solution.

WE DON'T GET TO THE UNDERLYING ISSUES AND THINKING. People often go into solution mode as soon as an issue is raised. Instead of making sure they understand the context, they try to solve things with limited information. This is especially tempting when someone asks a direct question. During a team workshop, a direct report asked her manager what he thought about a proposed departmental restructure. The manager began to explain why the new structure was better. When I asked the direct report what she thought, she expressed some insightful views and concerns that she had not felt comfortable voicing previously.

WE ASSUME THE ISSUE HAS BEEN THOUGHT THROUGH. People often raise issues or challenges that they haven't thought through. They may speak up just as a thought occurs to them without having taken time to think more about it. If we make the mistake of assuming their comment is well considered and move to solutions prematurely, we risk leaving the real issues unexplored.

WE ASSUME ADVICE IS WANTED. It is best not to assume people want your advice. They may want to think things out for themselves, or they may need a sounding board. It's difficult to think clearly when someone habitually tries to offer advice or tells you what they think before you've had a chance to finish your thought. One person put it this way: *There is a difference between 'I don't know what to do' and 'What should I do?'* In many circumstances, people just want to complain or express their feelings without 'closing' the issue with a solution.

NOT QUESTIONING THE UNDERLYING ASSUMPTIONS. A group was having a discussion about the format of their meetings: *Should we have them weekly, or maybe have a monthly meeting with the larger team, or have a quarterly workshop?* Different views were voiced about each of these options. Suddenly, someone asked, *Do we need these meetings at all? Why do we have them?* These questions stopped the group in its tracks and created a different level of conversation that addressed the underlying assumptions. If someone hadn't asked these questions, a decision would have been made that may not have solved anything.

A Crucial Step Before Problem Solving

Our habitual reaction is to get a quick sense of a problem, issue, or challenge and then jump straight to a solution or explanation. We often miss an important intermediary step, one that often determines how effective solutions or responses are. I call this middle step the Exploration phase. To remind yourself to include this middle step, think ***PES: Problem, Exploration, Solutions.***

In her first coaching session, Kathryn said, *Some of my direct reports get jealous when I give interesting projects to others. I want you to help me manage their jealousy.* I asked some exploratory questions: *Why do you think they're getting jealous? Why aren't you giving them interesting projects? How clear do you think they are about why they're not getting these projects? How clear are they about what you expect?* It became obvious to us both that managing jealousy was not the real problem or solution. Kathryn left our session with an action plan that included talking separately to each of her direct reports about her expectations and the steps each needed to take if they were to be given interesting projects.

In *Time to Think,*[37] author Nancy Kline talks about the importance of creating the right conditions to encourage high-quality thinking in others. One of the most important of those conditions is giving people uninterrupted time to talk. As Kline says, the quality of attention that we give to someone directly affects the quality of that person's thinking. Returning to the ideas discussed for Tool #1 about identifying assumptions and beliefs, Kline has coined a term called 'Incisive Questions' – questions that remove restrictive assumptions to free up our thinking about issues. These questions target assumptions that block or limit the way we deal with issues and even the way we frame issues in the first place. An example is to ask an initial

question like *What are you assuming that is stopping you from finding an answer to this situation?* Once you have uncovered an assumption (such as not being in a position of power, or not trusting your team), you then ask an incisive question that removes that block — *If you were in a position of power, what would you do? Or if you trusted your team completely, how would you act differently?*

In your work life, there are numerous opportunities to inquire and learn about what other people are thinking. Not doing so means losing the chance to find new ways of seeing things — and that means losing a chance to innovate. Even more important, making opportunities to help others think for themselves and explore the depth and breadth of factors influencing the issues they face often leads to breakthrough conversations, solutions and performance.

EXPLORING BEFORE PROBLEM SOLVING

❶ **CHECK DRIVERS.** It can be very useful to ask at the beginning of a discussion what people would like from you: *What sort of input are you looking for from me?* or *How are you hoping I can help?* Even if they don't know the answer, it gets them thinking about what's driving their behavior. It also helps to reflect and keep a check on what your drivers are in how they influence the way you interact during the conversation. Examples of drivers that may be worth examining are: having to be right, wanting to 'rescue' or blame the person, and controlling the direction of the conversation.

❷ **IDENTIFY/ EXPLORE ISSUES BROADLY AND DEEPLY.** Flushing out as much information as possible can minimize the tendency to go into explanation or solution mode too quickly. It also minimizes the risk of you doing all the work as solutions often become clearer when issues are explored! Try exploratory questions like *Tell me all the things that bother you about this?* Or *let's write down all the challenges first before starting to solve them* or *what has been the impact of each of these factors?* Asking *What else?* more than once can ensure that people get to say all they need to about an issue. In a way, you're trying to uncover the knowledge (and solution) that already resides in the other person by asking a range of questions. A more specific example is: *How have you handled situations similar to this current one?*[38]

❸ **CHECK PEOPLE'S MEANING OF WORDS.** Check people's definitions. Finding out what people actually mean by the words they use will often give you further insight. Ask questions like *If I were leading the team better, what would that look like to you? or When you talk about conflict, what do you mean?*

❹ **SUMMARIZE ALONG THE WAY TO HELP CLARIFY.** Periodically stating what you understand thus far can give everyone a chance to pause and reflect and to check that they have a common understanding. Before proceeding to solutions, summarize and ask questions that check your understanding: *What I think you are saying is that you're not happy in your position because you don't have enough responsibility and to you, responsibility means being able to make more decisions without having to check with me. Do I have that right?*

❺ **MANAGING UPWARD: IF YOU DON'T AGREE OR UNDER-STAND, ASK QUESTIONS.** You might feel more comfortable using tentative language when questioning a superior: *I'm not sure I understand the decision. Can you tell me more about the assumptions behind it? Or, can you tell me what would be an ideal outcome for you if money (time, resources, etc.) were no object?*

Get in the habit of exploring before seeking solutions. Taking the time to do so will help you arrive at more thoughtful, well-considered solutions and will facilitate more dynamic and potent conversations. Speaking of powerful conversations, there's nothing like being in a workplace culture of open feedback discussions to foster continued improvement of the way you lead and the way your team functions and performs.

⑥ **VIRTUAL TEAMS: REMEMBER THAT UNDERNEATH A QUESTION THERE IS OFTEN AN OPINION OR ASSUMPTION.** Brief interactions, without face-to-face contact, increase the chances of skimming over issues. For example, someone might ask who else is going to be involved in the project. Before moving to a solution or quick answer, it can be very enlightening to ask questions like: *What is on your mind? What are your views about this? Who would you like to see work on this project?* Probing for an underlying opinion behind a question can uncover the real reason for the question and perhaps uncover relevant information or assumptions. You might assign one team member to be a 'process observer' for each virtual meeting in order to have at least one set of ears focusing on the questions or assumptions behind the questions.

⑦ **CROSS-CULTURAL TEAMS: ADAPT TO CULTURAL DIMENSIONS RELATED TO STATUS, INFORMATION SHARING AND DECISION MAKING**. Some cultures believe that vigorous conversation is a sign of respect. Other cultures want to hold those types of conversations in private 'offline' meetings only with people they have established relationships with. Still others expect superiors to tell them what to do and how to do it. Some cultures want many details and data; others want information in bullet points. Individualistic cultures, where the interests of the individual override the interests of the group, tend to make quick decisions while more collectivistic cultures, where people are loyal to strong groups, take longer to make some decisions. These are a few of the areas to be aware of when exploring issues and making decisions with people from other cultures. Two useful questions to ask are: *How do you typically handle this sort of issue or decision?* and *Who else should we make sure we talk to about this before proceeding?*

Tool 8... Foster A Performance Feedback Culture

Alex, a senior manager, recalls his experience of reading the written comments from his direct reports in a leadership feedback report.

I had no idea that some of my direct reports were so affected by my style. It's hard to ignore what they wrote — that they felt patronized, reprimanded or put-down sometimes by the way I talked to them. That was one of those lightening bolt moments that you don't get often in your life. It was the beginning of taking a hard look at myself and changing the way I managed people.

A team leader, Lucy, talks about a significant conversation she had with a mentor. *I was going through a very challenging period at work. My manager*

• • • > Receiving honest feedback can be a challenging and infrequent event. As a result, people often miss out on important feedback about their performance, how they behave and affect other people, and their impact on achieving business results.

was never around, I had the team from hell and a lot of pressure from the business to hit high targets. I just accepted it all for a very long time and thought there was something wrong with me for not being able to handle things better. I decided to have a chat with someone who is a mentor and quickly realized how much I needed someone to confirm that I was doing a good job despite being in an impossible situation. It just took that little bit of feedback to validate that I was putting up with a bad situation for me to finally do something about it.

Chris and Simon are team members. Chris talks candidly about Simon during an initial coaching session. *Simon's very bright and brings in a lot of money for the business but he's not good at managing people. His direct reports come to me every day asking questions and needing direction. I'm sick of doing his job and trying to excuse his behavior. It's not my place to tell him. Anyway, they're supposed to be getting a replacement for his role but this has been supposed to happen for the last year.*

The first two scenarios are examples of the power of receiving feedback. Alex began to change his behavior after accepting the feedback in his report and Lucy decided to be proactive after her mentor gave her feedback about how he saw her situation. On the other hand, Chris' scenario is an example of the impact of a person not receiving feedback and this is, unfortunately, quite common in many organizations.

Even though most organizations have formal feedback processes (like annual reviews), receiving honest feedback about one's performance and behavior can be a challenging and infrequent event. As a result, people often miss out on important feedback about their performance, how they behave and affect other people, and their impact on achieving business results.

This has the potential to derail careers because relying on our own opinions about our performance is inadequate. We are not always aware of the difference with how we assess our own abilities compared to how others assess us. For example, studies showed that people were not very accurate in predicting their emotional intelligence scores[39] or in rating their leadership performance compared to how others rated them.[40]

Performance Feedback Involves Everyone

Performance feedback is a critical aspect of a leader's role. With the increased use of cross-functional teams, performance feedback can also be expected from team members. So it has, in many ways, become 'everybody's' job. Performance feedback can focus on many areas including someone regularly not meeting deadlines, lack of teamwork, and unproductive communication styles. Even though there are some performance issues that should be addressed solely by a person's manager or team leader, there are many instances where performance feedback from peers and direct reports can be very helpful to a person's performance, self-awareness, and reputation.

One of the main reasons that giving performance feedback is a challenge is because it seems like a personal judgment of someone. When hesitating to give feedback, many often ask themselves the following questions:

- *How many times should I raise the same issue?*
- *Am I being too demanding?*
- *How much have I contributed to this?*
- *Have I given this person enough opportunity to show they can perform?*
- *How much do I give allowances for their personal situation at home?*
- *Is it really my job to tell them about their behavior?*
- *How will they react?*

> With the increased use of cross-functional teams, performance feedback can also be expected from team members. So it has, in many ways, become 'everybody's' job.

73

In the absence of a clear answer to these questions, managers and team members simply do tasks themselves or avoid or delay talking about performance challenges in the hope that they'll improve or disappear. In most cases, performance issues don't improve or disappear; and often become worse. As in Chris' scenario, managers and team members like Simon can be in their roles for a very long time without knowing what people really think about them. There are several reasons for this.

The Challenge Of Giving Performance Feedback

NEGATIVE RESPONSE TO FEEDBACK. You only have to respond negatively to feedback once for people to be wary about a repeat experience. The most common example of this is when people don't reflect on how they contribute to situations and blame others for events or relationship issues. Sue had this experience with a colleague early in her career. The colleague begged her to tell her why people seemed to be put off by her style. Sue hesitated but finally described to her colleague her observations. Her colleague then coolly said, *You are obviously jealous of me.*[41]

PEOPLE ASSUME YOU MUST ALREADY KNOW. Sometimes people don't bother giving you important feedback because they assume you must know. Managers and team members can also miss out on positive feedback because people assume they would already know they are good at what they do. I have witnessed many managers' and team members' grateful (and sometimes teary) reactions to getting positive feedback from their colleagues. In some of these cases, they were receiving positive feedback for the very first time.

FEAR OF CONSEQUENCES. People's fears of the consequences of giving honest feedback can be based on their past experiences elsewhere or their assumptions about how their feedback will be received by others. Common fears include damaging the relationship, being ignored or ridiculed, being fired, or being sidelined.

A client told me that she had been encouraged by her manager to give honest feedback to him during a team workshop. Her manager took the feedback badly. As she put it, *For months after that workshop, he kept bringing it up to punish me for daring to say he wasn't perfect. It really affected our relationship after that and the whole team says they'll never give him feedback again!* Even when giving positive feedback, some people can fear that the person receiving the feedback might become arrogant or allow it to 'go to their head.'

IT IS NOT ALWAYS EASY TO GIVE FEEDBACK. Giving feedback is uncomfortable for many people and they will try to avoid it. My experience tells me that people are much more likely to give constructive feedback within confidential and structured feedback processes where the risks and difficulties are minimized. Kerry worked in a small office where people gave feedback to each other once a year. At the end of each year, her manager expected all the employees to have one-hour feedback meetings with each other. Kerry said, *If our manager had not built in that simple structure, we wouldn't have done it. It gave us the opportunity to do it and we always had positive and developmental feedback to give to each other.* People are also more likely to give constructive feedback, and have it accepted, if they have the skills to do it.[42]

CONFUSING THE PERSON WITH THE BEHAVIOR. People are more threatened about feedback conversations if they think personalities or hard-to-change qualities will be discussed. Feedback is less threatening and more useful when it focuses on specific behaviors and skills and not on general statements about the person. Rather than just telling someone they are brilliant or terrible presenters, they understand more about themselves (and are more likely to repeat their behaviors) if you tell them about their ability to explain complex ideas in simple steps, their skill in giving relevant and interesting examples, and their talent for answering people's questions briefly.

> ● ● ● **>** It is vital to focus on ways to make any feedback conversation as simple and 'clean' as possible with both sides taking responsibility for their part in a performance issue.

BEING AN AUTHORITY FIGURE. Even if you think you're one of the 'gang' and don't want your direct reports to see you as 'management', the reality is that if you are management, you are in a position of authority. This means that some people will hesitate to be honest with you. People also tend to transfer dynamics they had with their parents onto other authority figures. Graham is a good example of this. He was a high potential manager who was easily able to say what he thought when he spoke with his peers, direct reports or customers. However, when it came to his boss he told me, *I always leave meetings feeling like I didn't say what I really wanted to say. I lose my confidence to speak up when I'm with him.* If people had a particularly punitive parent, this dynamic can also play out in their relationships with peers and direct reports where they may anticipate negative responses to any challenging feedback or demands they make.

There are many possible reasons why people avoid giving honest performance feedback to others. The fear of how people will respond to feedback is one of the most common. Therefore, it is vital to focus on ways to make any feedback conversation as simple and 'clean' as possible with both sides taking responsibility for their part in a performance issue. In particular, if we are aware of our influence on situations, we can minimize the chance of inadvertently exacerbating performance issues or 'contaminating' them by our own behaviors or attitudes.

Contribute Positively To Performance Situations

BE CLEAR ABOUT EXPECTATIONS AND RESPONSIBILITIES.

One reason people do not perform well is that the requests and deadlines asked of them were not clear in the first place. Managers and team members can also indirectly take the ownership of a task away from people. For example, a manager once said to me that she had told one of her direct reports several times over the last year to complete a (non-urgent) reporting document and it still hadn't been done. The manager finally decided to change tactics and asked more questions to find out why the document hadn't been completed, what he was going to do differently, and when she could expect it on her desk. She said that her questions — including the most challenging one, ***How much responsibility are you taking for this?*** — had the effect of putting the onus of responsibility back onto her direct report and challenging his excuses. The report was done the following day.

RECOGNIZE THAT PEOPLE NEED HELP OR FEEDBACK TO CHANGE. In a perfect world, our direct reports and team members are self-aware, mature, and can manage their performance, especially their relationships with others. I've often heard people say something along the lines of *They're grownups, they're getting paid lots of money, and they should be able to sort out their differences.* An example like this is of two team members who would only speak to each other when absolutely necessary. There were unresolved issues and misunderstandings from more than six months earlier and a low level of trust between them. Their manager had insisted that they work on their differences and they tried to resolve their conflicts with little change. Both team members believed that although they had not managed to improve their relationship that it was not affecting anyone else. However, during a team-building workshop it became clear that their relationship dynamics were having a striking effect on the team's morale even though no one had said anything to them. If the team had not had a formal workshop with this critical peer feedback, the situation would have continued. It was only then that the two agreed to do more work to resolve their differences. They explored two areas in particular including how their conflict had first begun and what assumptions they were operating from. Once they began having an honest conversation, they realized that they had made negative assumptions about each other's motives and had distanced themselves from each other early on so that no further clarification of issues could take place.

FOCUS ON DEVELOPMENT AND LEARNING. A crucial part of a leader's role is to develop his or her people. Yet, for many this is a low priority. Instead of seeing an opportunity for growth, they may interpret a direct report's development needs as evidence of incompetence. When performance issues occur, this attitude fuels the tendency to blame individuals and to view performance problems and challenges as a chore. Team members can also have this same attitude toward each other rather than working together to learn from each other and to help each other grow.

SEEK SUPPORT. Even though managers and team members can receive support from various sources — training, colleagues, coaching — they are often likely to operate alone when it comes to managing performance issues. For some, the most help they receive from their colleagues or boss is a reminder that their direct report or team member is causing problems and that this should be addressed immediately. They may not have developed the skills or confidence to take part in robust performance feedback conversations and may need to ask others for advice or suggestions on how to best give and receive feedback. Seeking support may also involve increasing their understanding of their own and others' tendencies to take feedback personally and to react negatively, and strategies to manage this.[43]

The more you understand the challenges and benefits of giving and receiving feedback, and how to manage your own and others' responses to feedback, the more competent and confident you'll feel to promote regular feedback conversations that make a difference.

> • ▪ > Instead of seeing an opportunity for growth, they may interpret a direct report's development needs as evidence of incompetence.

FOSTERING A PERFORMANCE FEEDBACK CULTURE

❶ ACCEPT THAT DIGESTING FEEDBACK TAKES TIME.
It is useful to remind yourself and others about the corresponding emotional process that goes with performance feedback conversations, especially formal ones. Some common responses for managers and team members are to feel disappointed, pleasantly surprised or to challenge the feedback when they initially receive it. After an hour their response changes, as it does after sleeping on it, and again after a week of thinking about it. Some emotions that surface are similar to the grieving cycle such as shock, anger, denial, and acceptance.[44] It is advisable not to make any drastic life changes in the first 24 hours!

❷ PUT YOURSELF IN OTHERS' SHOES. Reflect on what you think your boss, peers, customers, clients, and direct reports would say about you to others. Showing that you have an idea of how people see you can make it easier for them to give you feedback. If they're hesitant, you could help them by saying something like, ***Please tell me if you think that I'm being too demanding.*** Or you could ask them directly: ***If you were going to tell someone what it's really like to work with me, what would you tell them?*** This is also a good question to ask your direct reports and team members when helping them to reflect on themselves: ***What do you think your peers (or another group) would say about you if they were describing your working style to others?***

❸ LISTEN BEFORE RESPONDING. It can be challenging to sit quietly and listen to feedback without disagreeing, justifying, or blaming others. Building in a framework of the four A's — Aware, Ask, Acknowledge, Action — when giving and receiving feedback can minimize these kinds of reactions. Allow yourself to become more aware of what others think by listening. Ask questions to clarify and ensure you understand the other person's perspective before responding: ***Tell me more about how it affects you when I do that*** or ***What's the impact on you?*** or ***What else do you need to tell me?*** Acknowledge aspects of the feedback to show you understand what the person thought or felt. Don't neglect to acknowledge your contribution to situations; it will help make the exchange a satisfying one. Acknowledge the person's effort and the time taken to give you feedback. Finally, tell the person what action you are planning to take; this might simply be that you'll reflect on the feedback over the coming week and meet again.

❹**USE MORE OF, LESS OF, AND SAME STATEMENTS.** Telling a colleague what you'd like them to do more of, less of, and what you'd like them to keep doing to help you to be most effective in your job can be very powerful feedback. Adding a sentence at the end of each statement explaining what your reciprocal action will be can be even more potent — it emphasizes your commitment to working together and taking responsibility. ***I'd like you to be less***

negative about new ideas I suggest to you. When you say my ideas are not going to work, it tends to demotivate me and I feel less positive about talking to you. If you're open to it, I'm willing to give you feedback when you do this. What do you think?

❺ **MANAGE UPWARD: POSITION FEEDBACK CONVERSA-TIONS FIRST.** Perhaps one of the most challenging feedback situations is giving feedback to a superior. How you position giving feedback is a critical first step. Try something like this: ***If***

I have any insights or feedback that I think might be useful to you, how would you feel about that and how would you like me to tell you? Once there's an agreement to have mutual feedback conversations, it can also be useful to agree on a structure for those conversations. Some people find SOS useful: Describe *specific* behaviors (for instance, giving only an hour's notice before a meeting); then describe the *outcome* of that behavior on you, others, and the business (inadequate preparation for the meeting, important details missing from the discussion, pressure on the rest of the day's work); and end with *suggestions* for alternative actions (prefer a day's notice).

❻ VIRTUAL TEAMS: CREATE A FEEDBACK CULTURE FROM THE START. Because of their nature, virtual teams may find themselves focusing on the task more than building relationships with, or giving feedback to other team members. This can increase the sense of isolation of remote members. Take at least ten minutes each week to give recognition to other team members. Focus on specific things members did to help achieve the team's goal. Or focus on one team member a week, giving feedback on what the members see as his or her strengths. Or create an 'appreciation board' in the team's virtual meeting room, posting specific feedback on members' contributions. If you have negative or developmental feedback for other team members, call them to discuss it live.

❼ CROSS-CULTURAL TEAMS: ADJUST THE FOCUS OF FEEDBACK CONVERSATIONS. Giving and receiving performance feedback is an area where cultures can differ markedly. It is important to ask questions that highlight these differences and clarify what meaningful feedback looks like within a person's culture. Ann Houston Kelley,[45] a consultant specializing in cross-cultural coaching with executives, suggests some useful questions to ask:
• *In what situations does feedback happen?*
• *Who can give feedback and who can receive it?*
• *How is a feedback process introduced and structured?*
• *What is the most acceptable ratio of positive feedback to negative feedback?* For example, some cultures prefer a balance of positive and negative feedback while others might prefer only positive feedback.

Being a savvy leader is about being open to all the possible forms of feedback or information that are available to us — from our thoughts, feelings, values and behaviors and others' behaviors, responses, attitudes to the many factors in our environment. More than ever before, employees have high expectations of work-life balance, meaningful work, opportunities to develop and grow, a chance to make a difference, satisfying work relationships and an organization that demonstrates corporate responsibility and sustainability. People skills are an integral part of being able to deliver on these demands and to attract, develop and retain talented people.

The more we try to understand others, and ourselves the more likely we are to make skillful decisions about how we manage ourselves and the situations and relationships we are in. We will then have greater impact on the people we work with, on work performance and on the wider environment and world in which we live. Creating more savvy leaders begins with you!

About the Author

Katina Cremona
Corporate and coaching psychologist

 Katina Cremona is a corporate psychologist who has worked in a clinical practice and as an executive coach, organization development consultant and facilitator over the last twenty-three years. She has extensive experience working nationally and internationally with senior managers of global corporations. Over this time, she has facilitated a large number of leadership, team development, and cultural change programs. Her broad range of industry clients include Diageo, GlaxoSmithKline, BNP Paribas and Microsoft.

Throughout her career, Katina has specialized in one-on-one sessions and has a passion for developing individuals to perform at their best in their professional and personal lives. She has worked with diverse individuals, teams and organizations, from senior executives to prison officers and fire-fighters. Katina's approach incorporates her extensive training and experience in understanding how people and systems develop and change.

Katina's educational background includes qualifications in psychology, teaching and acting. She has also completed numerous post-graduate trainings in areas such as mediation, group and organizational dynamics, psychotherapy, business and coaching. Katina is a member of the British Psychological Society and the Australian Psychological Society, and currently lives in Athens, Greece.

You can reach Katina by email at katina@katinacremona.com.

Acknowledgments

I would like to thank all my past and present clients for the privilege of working with them. I learn so much from their honesty, openness, and trust in me. There would be no book if it weren't for our work together. In particular, I want to thank Diageo, whose corporate culture embodies the spirit of this book; Tool #2 was particularly inspired by my work with Diageo Australia. Many thanks to Margot Hennessy for brilliantly matchmaking us by introducing me into the organization many years ago.

A book remains only an idea if it can't find readers, and I have Sue Hammond, a dream publisher, to thank for committing to this project and helping me bring it to fruition. We were supported by a great team of people. I'd also like to thank Keith Bendis for his clever cartoons. A cadre of reviewers generously took the time to give essential feedback that resulted in a better book; there are many of them to thank: Jan Baker, Dana Barz, Victoria Baugh, Frederica L. Burnett, Kate Canas, Cara Dilling, Kathleen Duffy, Justin Gallagher, Gary Gilligan, Tom Green, John Hansen, Doug Hensch, Hank Jonas, Amy Levine, Stéphane Lhuiller, Nancy Polk, Denise Renter, Mike Staniford, and Gail Williams. I wish to thank additional reviewers who chose to remain anonymous and others who kindly read a final draft to provide a quote.

I owe a debt of gratitude to the many colleagues I've had the pleasure of working with on projects where we've shared our expertise and experiences. There are far too many people to name who have had an influence on me and on how I work, and who have supported me in different ways over the years. I am particularly indebted to Bill Wood for his valuable comments and encouragement in the initial stages of this project, to Anthony Howard for his friendship and support, and to David Holloway for his wise, funny advice and belief in the project.

A special mention goes to my friends and family: Judith Fox for her invaluable input, feedback, and support of my writing in general, Michael and Susan Spiropoulos for their enthusiasm and input into early chapters, Timothy Johnson-Newell and Caroline Coggins for offering me a writing space, Marie Mauzy for her gift as a photographer, and many other dear friends and family members for being part of this journey. A heartfelt thank you to Jack Papadopoulos, John Papadopoulos, and Sarah Morris for their many generosities that have allowed me more time to write and to make a smooth transition to Athens. Finally, for his unwavering support and belief in me, I thank my husband, Nick Papadopoulos.

Endnotes and Resources

Endnotes

[1] Albert Ellis and Robert A. Harper, A *New Guide to Rational Living* (California: Wilshire Book Company, 1961).

[2] Aaron T. Beck, *Love Is Never Enough* (London & New York: Penguin Books, 1989).

[3] Martin E. P. Seligman Ph.D., *Authentic Happiness* (Sydney: Random House, 2002).

[4] Barbara L. Fredrickson, "The value of positive emotions."*American Scientist 91* (2003): 330-335.

[5] Joseph Ciarrochi, Joseph P. Forgas and John D. Mayer, *Emotional Intelligence in Everyday Life* (USA: Psychology Press, 2001).

[6] For more discussion and strategies on this type of dynamic, see Jean-François Manzoni and Jean-Louis Barsoux, "The Set-Up-to-Fail Syndrome," *Harvard Business Review* (March-April 1998): 101-113. The authors have also written a book on the same subject.

[7] Initial research in this area was in teachers' expectations of pupils by Robert Rosenthal and Lenore Jacobson, *Pygmalion in the Classroom: Teacher expectations and pupil's intellectual development* (New York: Holt, Rinehart and Winston, 1968).

[8] Robert Hogan and Rodney Warrenfelz, "Educating the modern manager," *Academy of Management Learning and Education* 2 (2003): 74-78.

[9] BlessingWhite Inc. *Employee Engagement Report* (2006); quote on pg 3. www.blessingwhite.com

[10] Definition from Sue Annis Hammond, *Podcast on Five Critical Tips to Increase Trust at Work* (2007), www.thinbook.com

[11] See Wendy Levinson et al., "Physician-Patient Communication: The Relationship with Malpractice Claims Among Primary Care Physicians and Surgeons," *Journal of the American Medical Association* 277, 7 (1997): 553-559. Also see Nalini, Ambady et al., "Surgeons' tone of voice. A clue to malpractice history," *Surgery,* 132, I (2002): 5-9.

[12] Isabel Briggs Myers with Peter B. Myers, *Gifts Differing* (California: Davies-Black Publishing, 1980).

[13] See www.thinbook.com for purchase of an online DiSC style instrument.

[14] John M. Gottman Ph.D. and Nan Silver, *Seven principles for making marriage work* (London: Orion Books Ltd, 2000).

[15] Marcus Buckingham and Donald O. Clifton, *Now, Discover Your Strengths* (London: Simon & Schuster, 2004).

[16] Mind maps are diagrams with a central concept such as 'work' with branches for each sub-set of the central concept. Tony Buzan coined this term and has written many books on this and related topics, Tony Buzan, *Make the Most of Your Mind* (UK: Macmillan, 1981).

[17] Kim W. Chan and Renee Mauborgne, "Fair Process: Managing in the Knowledge Economy," *Harvard Business Review* (July/August 1997).

[18] Bob Dick, *Helping Groups to be Effective. Second edition* (Australia: Interchange, 1991).

[19] Carl R. Rogers, *On Becoming a Person: A Therapist's Guide to Psychotherapy* (London: Constable, 1967).

[20] For lists of excellent questions to explore cultural differences, see Susan C. Schneider and Jean-Louis Barsoux, *Managing Across Cultures. Second edition* (UK: Pearson Education Limited, 2003).

[21] John D. Mayer, Peter Salovey and David R. Caruso, *MSCEIT User's Manual* (Canada: Multi-Health Systems, 2002).

[22] David R. Caruso and Peter Salovey, *The Emotionally Intelligent Manager: How to develop and use the four key emotional skills of leadership* (San Francisco: Jossey-Bass, 2004).

[23] Nancy Kline, *Time to Think: Listening to Ignite the Human Mind* (London: Cassell Illustrated, 1999).

[24] For an overview of nonverbal communication, see Mark Hickson, Don W. Stacks and Nina-Jo Moore, *Nonverbal Communication: Studies and Applications. Fourth edition* (California: Roxbury, 2004).

[25] Paula J. Caproni, *The Practical Coach* (Upper Saddle River: Prentice Hall, 2001).

[26] S.L. Jarvenpaa and D.E. Leidner, "Communication and trust in global virtual teams," *Organizational Science,* 10, 6 (1999): 791-815.

[27] Paul Ekman, *Emotions Revealed: Recognising Faces and Feelings to Improve Communication and Emotional Life* (Canada: Owl Books, 2004).

[28] Fons Trompenaars and Charles Hampden-Turner, *Riding the Waves of Culture: Understanding Cultural Diversity in Business. Second edition* (London: Nicholas Brealey Publishing, 1997).

[29] Susan Scott, *Fierce Conversations: Achieving Success at Work and in Life, One Conversation at a Time* (London: Piatkus, 2002), quote on p. 6.

[30] Mark Hickson, Don W. Stacks and Nina-Jo Moore, *Nonverbal Communication: Studies and Applications. Fourth Edition* (California: Roxbury, 2004).

[31] Barbara Minto, *The Pyramid Principle. Third edition* (UK: Pearson Education Limited, 2002).

[32] David R. Caruso and Peter Salovey, *The Emotionally Intelligent Manager: How to develop and use the four key emotional skills of leadership* (San Francisco: Jossey-Bass, 2004).

[33] Susan K. Gerke and Linda V. Berens, *Quick Guide to Interaction Styles and Working Remotely: Strategies for Leading and Working in Virtual Teams* (USA: Telos Publications, 2003).

[34] Geert Hofstede and Gert Jan Hofstede, *Culture and Organizations: Software of the Mind* (USA: McGraw-Hill, 2005).

[35] Fons Trompenaars and Charles Hampden-Turner, *Riding the Waves of Culture: Understanding Cultural Diversity in Business. Second edition* (London: Nicholas Brealey Publishing, 1997).

[36] Geert Hofstede and Gert Jan Hofstede, *Cultures and Organizations: Software of the Mind* (USA: McGraw Hill, 2005).

37 Nancy Kline, *Time to Think: Listening to Ignite the Human Mind* (London: Cassell Illustrated, 1999).

38 This question is inspired by the Solutions Focus which emphasizes finding examples of what is already working and amplifying them, when dealing with change. See Paul Z. Jackson and Mark McKergow, *The Solutions Focus: The SIMPLE way to positive change* (London: Nicholas Brealey Publishing, 2002).

39 M.A. Brackett, S.E. Rivers, and S. Shiffman, "Relating emotional abilities to social functioning: A comparison of self-report and performance measures of emotional intelligence," *Journal of Personality and Social Psychology* 91, 4 (2006): 780-795.

40 R. Hogan, G. Curphy, and J. Hogan, "What we know about leadership," *American Psychologist* 49 (1994): 493-504.

41 See Jay M. Jackson and Myra H. Strober for more on the various ways people feel threatened and avoid receiving feedback. They also provide some adaptive techniques to respond to feedback differently.

42 See Jean-François Manzoni for more good tips to make feedback more acceptable to the receiver.

43 Authors, Robert B. Kaiser and Robert B. Kaplan discuss five common kinds of sensitivities in leaders such as being sensitive to disapproval or to authority figures. These kinds of sensitivities can result in people being defensive or reacting negatively to feedback.

44 Elizabeth Kubler-Ross is known for writing about the five stages of the grieving cycle. The grieving cycle can help to understand the emotions people experience in other related situations like receiving challenging feedback or adapting to change.

45 Ann Houston Kelley, "Coaching executives across cultures" in M. Kets de Vries, K. Korotov and E. Florent-Treacy (eds), *Coach and Couch: The Psychology of Making Better Leaders* (UK: Palgrave Macmillan, 2007).

Resources

Chris Argyris, Robert Putman and Diana McLain Smith, *Action Science* (San Francisco: Jossey-Bass, 1985).

Chris Argyris, *Knowledge for Action* (San Francisco: Jossey-Bass, 1993).

Marcus Buckingham and Curt Coffman, *First, Break all the rules. What the world's greatest managers do differently* (London: Simon and Schuster UK Ltd, 2000).

Sarah Edelman Ph.D., *Change Your Thinking. Second edition* (Sydney: ABC Books, 2002).

Barbara L. Fredrickson, "The role of positive emotions in positive psychology: The broaden-and-build theory of positive emotions," *American Psychologist* 56 (2001): 218-226.

Malcolm Gladwell, *Blink* (Australia: Penguin Group, 2005).

William B. Gudykunst and Stella Ting-Toomey, *Culture and Interpersonal Communication* (USA: Sage Publications, 1988).

Sandra Krebs Hirsh and Jean M. Kummerow, *Introduction to Type in Organisations. Third edition* (California: Consulting Psychologists Press, 1999).

G. Hofstede, *Culture's consequences: Comparing values, behaviors, institutions, and organizations across nations* (Thousand Oaks, CA: Sage, 2001).

Jay M. Jackman and Myra H. Strober, "Fear of feedback," *Harvard Business Review* (April 2003): 3-8.

Robert B. Kaiser and Robert B. Kaplan, "The Deeper Work of Executive Development: Outgrowing Sensitivities," *Academy of Management Learning and Education* 5, 4 (2006): 463-483.

Robert Kegan and Lisa Laskow Lahey, *How the Way We Talk Can Change the Way We Work* (San Francisco: Jossey-Bass, 2001).

Richard R. Kilburg, *Executive Coaching. Developing Managerial Wisdom in a World of Chaos* (Washington: American Psychological Association, 2000).

Elizabeth Kubler-Ross, *On Death and Dying* (UK: Routledge, 1973).

Max Landsberg, *The Tao of Coaching* (London: Profile Books, 1996).

Jessica Lipnack and Jeffrey Stamps, "Virtual teams: the new way to work." *Strategy and Leadership 27,* (January-February 1999): 14-19 in Joyce S. Osland, David A. Kolb and Irwin M. Rubin, *The Organizational Behavior Reader. Seventh edition* (New Jersey: Prentice-Hall, 2001).

Jean-François Manzoni, "A better way to deliver bad news," *Harvard Business Review* (September 2002): 4-8.

Albert Mehrabian, *Silent Messages: Implicit communications of emotions and attitudes* (California: Wadsworth, 1981).

John Newton, Susan Long and Burkard Sievers (eds), *Coaching in Depth. The Organizational Role Analysis Approach* (London: Karnac, 2006).

Anton Obholzler and Vega Zagier Roberts (eds), *The Unconscious at Work* (London: Routledge, 1994).

Kerry Patterson, Joseph Grenny, Ron McMillan and Al Switzler, *The Balancing Act* (USA: International Thomson Publishing, 1996).

Edgar H. Schein, *Organisational culture and leadership. Third edition* (San Francisco: Jossey-Bass, 2004).

Martin E.P. Seligman Ph.D., *Learned Optimism* (Sydney: Random House, 1990).

Peter M. Senge, *The Fifth Discipline* (Australia: Random House Australia Pty Ltd, 1992).

Peter M. Senge, Art Kleiner, Charlotte Roberts and Bryan J. Smith, *The Fifth Discipline Fieldbook* (London: Nicholas Brealey Publishing Limited, 1994).

Paul D. Tieger and Barbara Barron-Tieger, *The Art of SpeedReading People* (USA: Little, Brown and Company, 1998).

Hendrie Weisinger, *Emotional Intelligence at Work* (San Francisco: Jossey-Bass, 1998).

Gary A. Williams and Robert B. Miller, "Change the Way You Persuade," *Harvard Business Review* (May 2002): 3-11.

Websites

www.authentichappiness.org
(Dr Martin Seligman – Positive Psychology resources and questionaires)

www.ccl.org
(Centre for Creative Leadership – non-profit organization focused on leadership)

www.eiconsortium.org
(Research on emotional intelligence and organizations)

www.emotionaliq.org
(The ability model of emotional intelligence – MSCEIT - Mayer-Salovey-Caruso Emotional Intelligence Test)

www.mhs.com
(Multi-Health Systems – MSCEIT distributors)

www.mrg.com
(Management Research Group – research/publications on leadership)

www.paulekman.com
(Understanding facial expressions, emotions, and deception)

www.positivepsychology.org
(University of Pennsylvania Positive Psychology Center)

www.presence.net
(Presence – profound change in people, organizations and society

www.solonline.org
(Society for Organizational Learning)

www.thesolutionsfocus.com
(The Solutions Focus approach to change in organizations)

TrustTalk™

Giving you the language to talk about Trust and Collaboration

TrustTalk™ is a powerful tool for conducting a developmental dialogue about what a team needs to do to enhance and develop trust and collaboration.

Each of the 71 cards in the TrustTalk™ deck contains:

- An item from our research describing best practices of high performing teams

- 3 questions to use as conversations starters for team dialogue about the item

- 2 suggestions on what the team can do differently to create more trust

- 1 suggestion for the team leader to help the team create more team trust and collaboration

- A keyword or phrase to use to pair similar items

The cards are durable, colorful and sorted by dimension. Also available as an on online assessment.

Price: $75 per deck

Order Now!
toll free: 888.316.9544
www.thinbook.com

WEBINARS

Thin Books Delivered Live!

Thin Book Publishing provides cutting edge information on how organizations can be more successful. With limited training time and travel budgets, as well as the growth of virtual teams, we have adapted our content into one hour webinars. They are *thin books delivered live* because we take our very practical content and give you the latest examples, research and to-do's. Webinars are interactive so your questions are answered by our expert leaders.

Our webinars are different from others in that we do NOT use the class as a method to sell you books or services. The class is the product. You will be delighted by the amount of practical knowledge we can deliver in this medium.

How Does a Webinar work?

Classes are designed to be 55 minutes in length and is facilitated by one of our authors or associates. Our sessions are interactive, not just a 'download' of information. We prefer to answer your questions and hear your comments as we go through the material.

We offer public Webinars where anyone may register for a specific time and class. We also offer private webinars, scheduled at your convenience for your participants.

For more information
toll free: 888.316.9544
www.thinbook.com

Trust & Collaboration Assessments

Highly collaborative workplaces have high trust. What are the actual behaviors that create an environment of trust and collaboration? We've done the research and created two assessments you can use to measure the current levels of those behaviors in your team and organization.

Designed to be debriefed appreciatively, the items are positively worded. You can use the results to sustain current strengths and work on improving the areas that are not where you wish.

This is not a 'prescriptive tool'; it is an action research tool. Your team or organization uses the results to design your preferred future. The assessment items give you concrete and actionable language to address this complex issue. Use the results to create the definition of trust and collaboration that works for your culture and organizational environment.

How the Assessments work:
- Browser based, Easy to use
- Confidential: No one at your organization will see the individual results
- Easy to launch and cost effective.
- Complete report with graphs, keywords and ranking of all items.

For more information
toll free: 888.316.9544
www.thinbook.com